Assisted Suicide

Other Books in the Current Controversies Series

I Assisted Suicide

Noël Merino, Book Editor

GREENHAVEN PRESS
A part of Gale, Cengage Learning

GALE
CENGAGE Learning·

Detroit • New York • San Francisco • New Haven, Conn • Waterville, Maine • London

GALE
CENGAGE Learning·

Elizabeth Des Chenes, *Managing Editor*

© 2012 Greenhaven Press, a part of Gale, Cengage Learning

Gale and Greenhaven Press are registered trademarks used herein under license.

For more information, contact:
Greenhaven Press
27500 Drake Rd.
Farmington Hills, MI 48331-3535
Or you can visit our Internet site at gale.cengage.com

For product information and technology assistance, contact us at

Gale Customer Support, 1-800-877-4253
For permission to use material from this text or product, submit all requests online at www.cengage.com/permissions

Further permissions questions can be emailed to permissionrequest@cengage.com

Articles in Greenhaven Press anthologies are often edited for length to meet page requirements. In addition, original titles of these works are changed to clearly present the main thesis and to explicitly indicate the author's opinion. Every effort is made to ensure that Greenhaven Press accurately reflects the original intent of the authors. Every effort has been made to trace the owners of copyrighted material.

Cover image © Richard Levine/Alamy.

LIBRARY OF CONGRESS CATALOGING-IN-PUBLICATION DATA

Assisted suicide / Noël Merino, book editor.
p. cm. -- (Current controversies) Summary: "Assisted Suicide: This series covers today's most current national and international issues and the most important opinions of the past and present. The purpose of the series is to introduce readers to all sides of contemporary controversies"-- Provided by publisher.
Includes bibliographical references and index.
ISBN 978-0-7377-5612-8 (hardback) -- ISBN 978-0-7377-5613-5 (paperback)
1. Assisted suicide. 2. Assisted suicide--Social aspects. 3. Assisted suicide--Moral and ethical aspects. I. Merino, Noël.
R726.A8533 2012
362.28--dc23
2011041397

Printed in the United States of America
1 2 3 4 5   16 15 14 13 12

FD084

Contents

Chapter 2: Is Assisted Suicide Moral?

No: Assisted Suicide Does Not Lead to Abuses

Chapter 4: Does Assisted Suicide Work Well Where It Is Legal?

Yes: Assisted Suicide Works Well Where It Is Legal

Concerns about harms from legalizing assisted suicide have not materialized in Oregon, and in fact palliative care of patients has improved since passage of the Death with Dignity Act. As such, those who oppose assisted suicide must do so based on nonconsequential, rather than consequential, matters.

No: Assisted Suicide Does Not Work Well Where It Is Legal

Foreword

By definition, controversies are "discussions of questions in which opposing opinions clash" (*Webster's Twentieth Century Dictionary Unabridged*). Few would deny that controversies are a pervasive part of the human condition and exist on virtually every level of human enterprise. Controversies transpire between individuals and among groups, within nations and between nations. Controversies supply the grist necessary for progress by providing challenges and challengers to the status quo. They also create atmospheres where strife and warfare can flourish. A world without controversies would be a peaceful world; but it also would be, by and large, static and prosaic.

The Series' Purpose

The purpose of the Current Controversies series is to explore many of the social, political, and economic controversies dominating the national and international scenes today. Titles selected for inclusion in the series are highly focused and specific. For example, from the larger category of criminal justice, Current Controversies deals with specific topics such as police brutality, gun control, white collar crime, and others. The debates in Current Controversies also are presented in a useful, timeless fashion. Articles and book excerpts included in each title are selected if they contribute valuable, long-range ideas to the overall debate. And wherever possible, current information is enhanced with historical documents and other relevant materials. Thus, while individual titles are current in focus, every effort is made to ensure that they will not become quickly outdated. Books in the Current Controversies series will remain important resources for librarians, teachers, and students for many years.

In addition to keeping the titles focused and specific, great care is taken in the editorial format of each book in the series. Book introductions and chapter prefaces are offered to provide background material for readers. Chapters are organized around several key questions that are answered with diverse opinions representing all points on the political spectrum. Materials in each chapter include opinions in which authors clearly disagree as well as alternative opinions in which authors may agree on a broader issue but disagree on the possible solutions. In this way, the content of each volume in Current Controversies mirrors the mosaic of opinions encountered in society. Readers will quickly realize that there are many viable answers to these complex issues. By questioning each author's conclusions, students and casual readers can begin to develop the critical thinking skills so important to evaluating opinionated material.

Current Controversies is also ideal for controlled research. Each anthology in the series is composed of primary sources taken from a wide gamut of informational categories including periodicals, newspapers, books, US and foreign government documents, and the publications of private and public organizations. Readers will find factual support for reports, debates, and research papers covering all areas of important issues. In addition, an annotated table of contents, an index, a book and periodical bibliography, and a list of organizations to contact are included in each book to expedite further research.

Perhaps more than ever before in history, people are confronted with diverse and contradictory information. During the Persian Gulf War, for example, the public was not only treated to minute-to-minute coverage of the war, it was also inundated with critiques of the coverage and countless analyses of the factors motivating US involvement. Being able to sort through the plethora of opinions accompanying today's major issues, and to draw one's own conclusions, can be a complicated and frustrating struggle. It is the editors' hope that Current Controversies will help readers with this struggle.

Introduction

> "*The language used will not resolve the underlying controversy about whether or not helping someone die is moral, or should be legal.*"

Controversy over whether assisted suicide is ever justified is so deep that those with opposing views on the issue cannot even agree on the terminology to describe the practice. Understanding the terminology used by both sides helps to illuminate the moral and legal issues that are at stake and helps shed light on why people take different positions on this practice.

Assisted suicide, often called physician-assisted suicide, is when a physician or other person assists in the death of an individual who has expressed the desire to die. Assisted suicide is to be distinguished from the broader concept of euthanasia. Euthanasia is the practice of intentionally ending the life of another. A distinction can be drawn between passive and active euthanasia, with the latter considered more controversial than the former. Additionally, a distinction can be made between voluntary and involuntary euthanasia, with the latter considered much more controversial than the former.

Passive euthanasia describes a medical situation where treatment is withdrawn or withheld, ultimately leading to death. Many people who are ill make a decision to stop treatment at a certain point when death is inevitable. When a doctor follows the directive of the patient in this situation, it is a case of voluntary passive euthanasia. The difference between passive and active euthanasia is that in active euthanasia, death is brought about by an action rather than by the omission of treatment. For example, a terminally ill person may re-

quest a lethal dose of medication to hasten death. If a doctor were to then inject this person with a lethal dose of medicine—causing death—that would be a case of voluntary active euthanasia. Involuntary euthanasia—whether passive or active—describes a situation where consent for death is not given by a patient but is given by another individual, such as a family member or other caregiver; for that reason the practice is much more controversial, with many arguing that involuntary euthanasia is simply murder.

Assisted suicide is a situation that involves getting help in dying (such as providing a lethal dose of medicine), thus distinguishing it from an act of euthanasia where someone else performs an act (such as lethal injection) that does the killing. In this sense, assisted suicide is by its nature voluntary and active because the patient himself or herself must ultimately perform the act of taking his or her own life. Thus, the controversy about assisted suicide is about whether another person should be able to help someone die, rather than the broader question involved in euthanasia of whether a person should be able to actively kill someone.

The language used by the two sides on the issue of assisted suicide illustrates the depth of disagreement about the practice. Barbara Coombs Lee, president of Compassion & Choices—the leading advocate for state laws that permit doctors to help terminally ill patients end their lives—contends that *assisted suicide* is the wrong terminology. She says, "Our movement for end-of-life choice does not condone assisted suicide, and it never has." Lee prefers *aid in dying* as the proper term for the practice: "Doctors who acknowledge their patients' imminent death and accede to their thoughtful request are providing aid in dying, not assisted suicide." Dr. E. James Lieberman expresses the contrast between a suicidal person and a person who seeks aid in dying under Oregon's Death with Dignity Act (DWDA): "The suicidal patient has no terminal illness but wants to die; the DWDA patient has a terminal illness and wants to live." Lee contends that assisted suicide describes a criminal situation where, for example, someone helps a depressed teenager tie a noose in order to commit suicide. Aid in dying, by contrast, is when a physician helps a terminally ill, dying patient hasten death. She concludes, "The two situations are so different, it is impossible to use the same phrase to name them. Indeed, the crime is assisted suicide. The kindness is aid in dying."

Opponents of assisted suicide argue that attempts to eliminate the word *suicide* are simply word games intended to sway public opinion. Rita L. Marker and Wesley J. Smith of the Patients Rights Council—an organization that opposes assisted suicide—claim that the effort to change terminology shows that "the deconstruction of language, with disregard for facts and accurate definitions, is infecting medical and health-care ethics and policies." They claim that Compassion & Choices made the decision to change the terminology after research and polling "found that people have a negative impression of the term 'assisted suicide,' but, if euphemistic slogans like 'death with dignity' or 'end of life choices' were used to describe the same action, response was relatively positive." Bioethicist Daniel Callahan contends that the decision to title the legislation legalizing assisted suicide in both Oregon and Washington as The Death with Dignity Act, "is a flagrant cooptation of wording widely used to describe a peaceful death" and was coupled "with a deliberate attempt to avoid calling the proposed legislation 'physician-assisted suicide.'"

For the time being, most media outlets utilize the term *assisted suicide* to refer to the practice at issue. Whatever one calls the practice, the language used will not resolve the underlying controversy about whether or not helping someone die is moral, or that it should be legal. There is widespread disagreement about whether social acceptance of assisted suicide leads to abuses, and there are differing opinions about whether or not assisted suicide works well where it is legal.

These fascinating debates about assisted suicide are explored in *Current Controversies: Assisted Suicide.*

CHAPTER 1

Should Assisted Suicide Be Legal?

Overview: Americans' Views on Legalizing Assisted Suicide

David Masci

David Masci is a senior researcher at the Pew Research Center's Forum on Religion and Public Life, where he is the in-house expert on religion and science and such controversial issues as abortion, assisted suicide, and gay marriage.

Ten years ago this month [October 2007], Oregon enacted a law permitting physicians to prescribe a lethal dose of drugs to certain terminally ill patients, a practice often called physician-assisted suicide. . . .

The Debate About Assisted Suicide

Oregon's law applies only to patients who are terminally ill and likely to die within six months, a diagnosis that must be confirmed by two physicians. In addition, eligible patients must possess the mental capacity to give informed consent; cannot suffer from depression; and must sign a written declaration, in front of two witnesses, stating that they are mentally competent and acting voluntarily. Finally, while doctors may prescribe the lethal drugs, the dose must be administered by the patient. Between the time the statute was enacted in 1997 and the end of 2006, 292 terminally ill people had availed themselves of the right to end their lives, according to state records.

Opponents of physician-assisted suicide—including some medical groups, such as the American Medical Association; some disability-rights advocates; and some more socially conservative religious groups, such as the Roman Catholic Church,

David Masci, a portion of this article is based on "The Right-to-Die Debate and the Tenth Anniversary of Oregon's Death with Dignity Act," Pew Research Center's Forum on Religion & Public Life, © 2007, Pew Research Center. http://pewforum.org. All rights reserved. Reproduced by permission.

Orthodox Jews and evangelical Protestant denominations—argue that suicide is a tragedy, not a personal choice. Furthermore, they say, the practice will inevitably lead to abuses, such as patients who might be pressured to take their own lives by family members and others who wish to save money or end the burden of caring for someone with a debilitating illness. In addition, opponents say, doctor-assisted suicide devalues human life by sending a message to the broader culture that some people's lives are worth less than others. Finally, they contend, physician-assisted suicide is at the top of a very slippery slope that could eventually lead to involuntary euthanasia of people who are severely handicapped or infirm.

Polls show that the country is divided on the issue of physician-assisted suicide.

Supporters of the practice include some more socially liberal Christian and Jewish religious denominations, some civil rights groups and some organizations that advocate on behalf of the rights of patients, particularly the terminally ill. These groups and others argue that "physician aid in dying"—calling the practice "suicide" unfairly imbues it with negative connotations, they contend—is not about forcing or pressuring anyone but rather is about giving people with no hope of recovery the option to end their lives before their physical pain becomes unbearable or before they fully lose control of their mental faculties. In addition, supporters argue, giving people the option to end their suffering does not devalue human life. On the contrary, they say, physician aid in dying promotes human dignity by allowing those in the last stages of potentially painful and debilitating illnesses to end their lives on their own terms.

Public Opinion Is Divided

Polls show that the country is divided on the issue of physician-assisted suicide, although the numbers differ somewhat based on how the survey questions are worded. For instance, a July 2005 poll conducted by the Pew Research Center for the People & the Press and the Pew Forum on Religion & Public Life asked half the participants about their views on the issue using one question and asked the other half a differently worded question. The survey found that 44 percent of respondents favored making it legal for doctors to "assist terminally ill patients in committing suicide" when the question was worded this way. But support for the practice rose slightly, to 51 percent, when people were asked if they favor making it legal for doctors to "give terminally ill patients the means to end their lives."

The debate over the legal, ethical and political implications of death and dying is not new. But the modernization of health care in the 20th century dramatically changed the character of death and dying, and has cast this old debate in a different light. Beginning a little more than a century ago, people began to routinely die in hospitals rather than at home. More importantly, new technologies, such as the artificial respirator, allowed doctors to prolong life, often for substantial periods of time. At the same time, new drugs, such as morphine, allowed doctors to alleviate pain and to painlessly end patients' lives.

By the 1950s, a small body of writers and thinkers in the United States and Europe began to argue in favor of allowing patients' lives to be ended by the patients themselves, in the case of the terminally ill, or by their families and guardians, in the case of those on life support. These arguments gained wider acceptance in the 1960s as the civil rights movement, the sexual revolution and other social movements helped to expand notions of personal freedom.

In the 1970s the end-of-life debate vaulted onto the national stage thanks in large part to the highly publicized 1975 case of Karen Ann Quinlan, a 21-year-old New Jersey woman who had fallen into a coma and was judged to be in a "chronic persistent vegetative state," unable to survive without the help of an artificial respirator. Efforts by Quinlan's family to remove her life support were thwarted by her doctor, leading to a lawsuit and a ruling by the New Jersey Supreme Court that patients (and by extension their families) have a right to terminate life support.

Relevant Court Decisions

In 1990, the right-to-die debate reached the U.S. Supreme Court in a case involving Nancy Cruzan, who had been in a persistent vegetative state for five years when her parents asked that her feeding tube be removed. In *Cruzan v. Director, Missouri Department of Public Health*, the court, in a 5–4 decision, implicitly recognized for the first time a constitutional right to refuse treatment in extraordinary circumstances.

In some ways, *Cruzan* presaged another high-profile case, that of Terri Schiavo, the severely brain-damaged woman whose husband and legal guardian fought against her parents to remove the feeding tube that was keeping her alive. Schiavo became a national media story from 2003 to 2005, as those favoring the "right to die" and those favoring the "right to life" battled over her fate in the courts, in the court of public opinion and even in Congress. But throughout the struggle, courts consistently ruled that Schiavo's husband had the ultimate right to decide what his wife would have wanted, and with all appeals exhausted, she died on March 31, 2005, after her feeding tube was removed.

In the last decade, many of the high-profile battles over physician-assisted suicide have taken place in the courts.

In the years between the Cruzan and Schiavo cases, a number of states held referenda on legalizing physician-assisted suicide for certain terminally ill patients. Voters rejected such measures in Washington state in 1991 and in California the following year. [Washington did legalize physician-assisted suicide in 2008.] Although voters in Oregon first approved the Death with Dignity Act in 1994, it did not take effect until 1997, owing to court challenges and a second state referendum that unsuccessfully sought to nullify the act.

In the last decade [1997–2007], many of the high-profile battles over physician-assisted suicide have taken place in the courts. In 1997, the Supreme Court ruled in *Washington v. Glucksberg* that while the Constitution guarantees the right to refuse medical treatment, it does not give patients the right to assisted suicide. In 2006, the high court, in *Gonzales v. Oregon*, rejected an effort by the U.S. attorney general to use a federal drug law to prohibit doctors in Oregon from prescribing lethal doses of drugs to terminally ill patients under the Death with Dignity Act.

Supporters of physician-assisted suicide had hoped that the *Gonzales v. Oregon* decision would give their movement the momentum it needed to encourage other states to adopt laws similar to Oregon's Death with Dignity Act. But, as the recent defeat of a doctor-assisted suicide bill in California shows, opposition to the practice remains strong, even in a state with a reputation for being at the forefront of new social trends. [At the end of 2009, the Montana Supreme Court ruled that nothing prevented doctors from prescribing lethal drugs to terminally ill patients, essentially legalizing physician-assisted suicide in Montana.]

People Have the Right to Commit Suicide

Thomas Bowden

Thomas Bowden is an analyst focusing on legal issues at the Ayn Rand Center for Individual Rights in Washington, D.C.

Since 1997 Oregon physicians have been permitted by statute to help their patients commit suicide. On Tuesday [January 17, 2006], the Supreme Court upheld this controversial law [*Gonzales v. Oregon*], reaching the right result for the wrong reasons. By basing its decision on legal technicalities, the Court managed to avoid addressing the real issue: an individual's unconditional right to commit suicide.

Suicide in the Courts

The Oregon law permits a doctor to prescribe a lethal dose of drugs to a mentally competent, terminally ill patient who makes written and oral requests, consults two physicians, and endures a mandatory waiting period. The patient's relatives and doctors are powerless to engage in legalized "mercy killing," as they cannot apply on the patient's behalf, and the patient himself administers the lethal dose.

In 2001 Attorney General John Ashcroft decreed that any doctor prescribing such a dose would violate federal law against dispensing controlled dangerous substances without a "legitimate medical purpose." Consequently, the case reached the Supreme Court as a technical debate between federal and state governments over which one should regulate the practice of medicine. The Court ruled that the state of Oregon could permit assisted suicide, despite the federal law.

But who was missing from that debate? The individual patients whose lives were at stake.

Thomas Bowden, "Assisted Suicide: A Moral Right," *American Chronicle*, January 17, 2006. www.americanchronicle.com.

What the Supreme Court should have done was bypass legal technicalities and revisit its 1997 decision in *Washington v. Glucksberg*, which held that individuals have no constitutionally protected right of suicide, and hence no right to obtain assistance in that act.

There is no rational, secular basis upon which the government can properly prevent any individual from choosing to end his own life.

The Right to Life and Death

What the courts must grasp, if they are ever to resolve the battle over assisted suicide once and for all, is that there is no rational, secular basis upon which the government can properly prevent any individual from choosing to end his own life. When religious conservatives use secular laws to enforce their idea of God's will, they threaten the central principle on which America was founded.

The Declaration of Independence proclaimed, for the first time in the history of nations, that each person exists as an end in himself. This basic truth—which finds political expression in the right to life, liberty, and the pursuit of happiness—means, in practical terms, that you need no one's permission to live, and that no one may forcibly obstruct your efforts to achieve your own personal happiness.

But what if happiness becomes impossible to attain? What if a dread disease, or some other calamity, drains all joy from life, leaving only misery and suffering? The right to life includes and implies the right to commit suicide. To hold otherwise—to declare that society must give you permission to kill yourself—is to contradict the right to life at its root. If you have a duty to go on living, despite your better judgment, then your life does not belong to you, and you exist by permission, not by right.

For these reasons, each individual has the right to decide the hour of his death and to implement that solemn decision as best he can. The choice is his because the life is his. And if a doctor is willing to assist in the suicide, based on an objective assessment of his patient's mental and physical state, the law should not stand in his way.

Religion and the Law

Religious conservatives' outrage at the Oregon law stems from the belief that human life is a gift from the Lord, who puts us here on earth to carry out His will. Thus, the very idea of suicide is anathema, because one who "plays God" by causing his own death, or assisting in the death of another, insults his Maker and invites eternal damnation, not to mention divine retribution against the decadent society that permits such sinful behavior.

If [President] George W. Bush were to contract a terminal disease, he would have a legal right to regard his own God's will as paramount, and to instruct his doctor to stand by and let him suffer, just as long as his body and mind could endure the agony, until the last bitter paroxysm carried him to the grave. But the Bush administration has no right to force such mindless, medieval misery upon doctors and patients who refuse to regard their precious lives as playthings of a cruel God.

Conservatives crave to inject religion into the bloodstream of American law, thereby assisting in our own national suicide. However, they cannot succeed without the Supreme Court's consent. Sooner or later, the Court must confront the main issue, and decide whether an individual's right to life includes the right to commit suicide.

Physician-Assisted Death Should Be a Last Resort Option

Timothy E. Quill

Timothy E. Quill is a professor at the University of Rochester School of Medicine and Dentistry and director of the Center for Ethics, Humanities, and Palliative Care.

Although there has been relatively little activity in the last ten years with regard to legal access to physician-assisted death, this fall [2008] a citizens' initiative in the state of Washington is proposing an Oregon-style law that would allow legal access to potentially lethal medication for terminally ill patients, subject to defined safeguards. As the rhetoric inevitably heats up, this seems like a good time to review areas of progress in palliative and end-of-life care and to consider whether laws like the one on the table in Washington are either needed or desirable.

Several things are clear: (1) Palliative care and hospice have improved in terms of access and delivery, and they remain the standards of care for addressing the suffering of seriously ill patients. (2) Despite state-of-the-art palliative measures, there will remain a relatively small number of patients whose suffering is insufficiently relieved. (3) Several "last resort" options, including aggressive pain management, forgoing life-sustaining therapies, voluntarily stopping eating and drinking [VSED], and sedation to unconsciousness to relieve otherwise intractable suffering, could address many of these cases. The question remains as to whether physician-assisted death— that is, providing terminally ill patients with a potentially lethal prescription that they could ingest on their own to relieve

Timothy E. Quill, "Physician-Assisted Death in the United States: Are the Existing 'Last Resorts' Enough?," *Hastings Center Report*, vol. 38, no. 5, September/October 2008. All rights reserved. Reproduced by permission.

otherwise intractable suffering by directly hastening death—should be one of these last resort options.

My own answer to this last question is a cautious "yes": open access to physician-assisted death, subject to the safeguards of excellent palliative care and access to other last resort options, gives patients an important additional option, and the benefits of legalization outweigh the risks.

Progress in Palliative Care

Perhaps the most dramatic sign of progress has been the coming of age of the palliative care movement, which allows fully informed decision-making and the provision of treatments to maximize quality of life for all seriously ill patients alongside any and all disease-directed treatment that patients want to continue. Almost all major medical centers now have inpatient palliative care consultation services, and similar services are spreading into community hospitals. Consultation possibilities are also spreading into the outpatient and home settings, although the gaps between need and availability are much wider in these contexts. The American Board of Medical Specialties has recently given palliative care the status of being a board-certified subspecialty, and fellowship programs are sprouting up across the country.

Open access to physician-assisted death ... gives patients an important additional option, and the benefits of legalization outweigh the risks.

There remain serious challenges. There are not enough skilled palliative care clinicians to meet the growing needs, and reimbursement for palliative care services—which rely heavily on counseling and coordination of care rather than expensive procedures—remains problematic. Similar gaps exist in providing basic palliative care education for all clinicians who care for seriously ill patients, and in generating an evidence base for the field. Nonetheless, palliative care seems to have passed the "tipping point" as a field; most patients and families can find the treatments that they need regardless of their stage of disease.

A Growth in Hospice Programs

When patients become terminally ill, access to palliative care is facilitated by the proliferation of hospice programs. Hospice remains our premiere program to provide palliative care for terminally ill patients who are willing to forgo further treatment of their underlying disease, as it provides, pays for, and coordinates comprehensive quality-of-life-oriented treatments for terminally ill patients. Hospice has expanded considerably in the last ten years, primarily in two domains: the inclusion of terminally ill patients with diseases other than cancer—congestive heart failure, dementia, and chronic lung disease, for example—and the ability to supplement the palliative aspects of care for terminally ill patients who reside in skilled nursing homes.

Even with the best possible palliative care, there will always be a small percentage of cases where suffering sometimes becomes unacceptably severe.

Despite this progress, the majority of patients who die in the United States are never transitioned to hospice, mostly because of a requirement that once they are in hospice they will forgo disease-directed therapy. Some larger hospices are experimenting with loosening these restrictions through "bridge" programs that let patients continue active treatments that are important to them and have some potential for helping while at the same time receiving the full benefits of hospice. Since hospices are paid on a per diem basis (on average, about $135 per day), only the very large, affluent hospices can afford to offer expensive disease-directed therapy at the same time that they are providing and paying for comprehensive palliative care, but there is much more flexibility and willingness to experiment with these areas now than ten years ago.

Significant progress has also been made in the articulation and provision of last resort options for patients whose suffering becomes unacceptable to them despite state-of-the-art palliative care. Ten years ago, the problem of intractable suffering was often not acknowledged or was blamed on the clinician ("They don't have adequate expertise") or the patients ("They want too much control over their fate"). Now, it is much more widely acknowledged that even with the best possible palliative care, there will always be a small percentage of cases where suffering sometimes becomes unacceptably severe, and that clinicians are obligated to treat these circumstances as a palliative care emergency that requires consultation and committed efforts to respond in the most helpful, least harmful way.

Uncontroversial Last Resort Options

When unacceptable suffering persists for terminally ill patients despite state-of-the-art palliative care, four options have emerged as last resort possibilities. The first two are widely accepted and relatively uncontroversial:

Right to intensive pain and symptom management. Pain can almost always be sufficiently relieved without any significant risk of hastening death, but there will be a few cases where pain accelerates severely toward the very end of life and pain medicines must be proportionately increased, bringing an increasing risk of hastening death. Patients and families, having given their informed consent, should be able to count on their doctors' willingness to take these risks as part of their commitment to relieve suffering, and medical ethics and law stand firmly behind this commitment.

Consider a case like this: a patient with advanced bladder cancer is nearing death and must make daily tradeoffs between adequate pain relief and sedation. She reaches a point where she "just wants to be out of pain." After extensive discussion with patient and family, her dose of opioids is gradually increased until her pain is sufficiently relieved, but after that point she eats and drinks very little and sleeps most of the time. She dies a week and a half later. Although death may have been unintentionally hastened by a small amount, in this process the obligation to relieve her severe suffering warranted taking that risk.

Some patients suffer unacceptably from symptoms other than pain, and their lives (and deaths) are not directly dependent on life-sustaining technologies.

Right to forgo life-sustaining therapy. Medicine has made great strides in prolonging life, and a small but significant part of this progress has been the availability of life-sustaining technologies. These technologies no longer just mean ventilators and feeding tubes; they now include radical technologies such as ventricular-assist devices. But while the array of medical choices faced by patients and families has grown more complex, ethics and law remain clear that patients have a right both to forgo such treatments and to stop them once started. Here's a typical case that turns on this kind of decision: an elderly man fractures his spine falling off a ladder. He initially accepts intubation and surgery in hope that he will recover neurological function, but four weeks later, he has not. He cannot imagine living this way, and after extensive discussions with his medical team and his family, he is mildly sedated and removed from the ventilator. He dies within twenty-four hours.

Complex Last Resort Options

Of course, some patients suffer unacceptably from symptoms other than pain, and their lives (and deaths) are not directly dependent on life-sustaining technologies. A portion of these patients look for options to escape suffering and even hasten death by means other than physician-assisted death. Two additional possibilities have emerged over the past decade. While clearly more morally complex and less settled than the first two options, these options seem to generate less legal and ethical controversy than physician-assisted death:

Voluntarily stopping eating and drinking. VSED is different from the natural loss of interest in food and drink that occurs when a person is actively dying. It is an informed decision to stop food and fluids while one is still physically capable in an effort to hasten death and escape suffering. The decision is entirely within the patient's control, but it requires considerable resolve, since the patient generally continues to live for one to two weeks after stopping. Although VSED is not directly "physician-assisted," it needs to be "physician-supported": the patient must be assessed at the outset to ensure that he or she is competent and has adequate palliative care, and the physician must help the patient and family to address any unforeseen complications as the process unfolds.

VSED is only an option when the patient retains mental capacity. Suppose, for example, that a patient with amyotrophic lateral sclerosis has become tired of living in the circumstances imposed by his illness. He does not want a feeding tube or a mechanical ventilator, and he feels that he is dying too slowly. He asks about physician-assisted death. After careful assessment of his capacity and motivation, his physician raises the possibility of VSED. Since eating and drinking are already a daily struggle, he and his family welcome this alternative. His family can then come together for his last two weeks, during which he will be supported by home hospice. In the final phase of this process, he may be mildly delirious because of the metabolic changes of dehydration, but usually these and other symptoms can be well managed as part of his hospice support.

Sedation to unconsciousness. This type of sedation is distinct from the proportionate use of sedatives to treat severe anxiety or delirium, which is a relatively common part of terminal care. Instead, it is an explicit decision to render the patient unconscious so that he or she can escape otherwise severe and intractable suffering. Other potentially life-prolonging treatments such as food and fluids are usually discontinued at the same time. There is general agreement on its use as a last resort to relieve severe, intractable suffering in imminently dying patients, but as one gets further away from these circumstances, agreement about its permissibility falls off sharply.

There are ... data from Oregon to suggest that the legalization of physician-assisted death enhances rather than undermines other aspects of palliative and end-of-life care.

Consider an elderly holocaust survivor dying of end-stage congestive heart failure who was transferred to an acute hospice/palliative care unit to manage his terminal shortness of breath. The opioids used to treat his dyspnea made him delirious, and he began having flashbacks from his time in the concentration camps. Usual sedatives did not control his agitation, and family and staff agreed that this suffering was unacceptable, so he was sedated to unconsciousness with phenobarbitol. The dose was adjusted until he appeared to be resting comfortably, but he was completely unresponsive. Artificial hydration and nutrition were not provided, with the family's consent. His level of sedation was maintained until he died seventy-two hours later.

The Empirical Data from Oregon

By far the best data about physician-assisted death in the United States come from Oregon, where the practice is reported to the health department and where annual summaries have been prepared every year since legalization. The practice has been remarkably stable over the ten intervening years, accounting for approximately one out of every thousand deaths per year. This appears to be a very small number given the amount of controversy surrounding the practice, but one in fifty patients talk to their doctor about it, and one in six talk with family members, suggesting that the *availability* of such an escape may be much more important to many patients than its actual use. The Oregon statute requires that patients be informed of "feasible alternatives," including hospice and palliative care and other last resort alternatives, and some choose alternatives other than physician-assisted death.

There are also data from Oregon to suggest that the legalization of physician-assisted death enhances rather than undermines other aspects of palliative and end-of-life care. Oregon has one of the highest rates of hospice referral in the nation, and the vast majority of patients who choose physician-assisted death are simultaneously enrolled in hospice. Oregon also has relatively high rates of opioid prescription per capita, and physicians as well as other medical professionals have very high rates of attending training courses in both palliative care and end-of-life medical decision-making. There is also a statewide form, "Physician Orders for Life-Sustaining Treatment" (POLST), for recording a patient's wishes about cardiopulmonary resuscitation and other potentially life-sustaining therapies. The form has become a model for other states. Overall, Oregon appears to be among the leaders in comparison to other states in virtually all aspects of palliative and end-of-life care, including allowing open access to physician-assisted death, subject to safeguards.

Illegal Physician-Assisted Death

The secret practice of physician-assisted death in the rest of the nation is very difficult to study. To admit to participation, a physician has to admit to a crime, and along with any family present, runs the risk of prosecution. On the other hand, there appears to be very little interest in prosecuting such cases providing they are not discovered or flaunted, leading to a "don't ask, don't tell" policy that is unpredictable and potentially dangerous. Under this policy, there is no opportunity to get second opinions from experts in palliative care, no documentation, and considerable potential for idiosyncratic responses from clinicians.

In the mid-1990s, I was part of a team that conducted an empirical study of the secret practice, using research techniques that protected anonymity. We found that physician-assisted death and euthanasia accounted for approximately 1 to 2 percent of deaths. Although this appears to be ten to twenty times higher than the rates reported in Oregon, the reporting techniques were so different that the rates are not directly comparable. On the other hand, we know from Oregon that conversations with doctors about these issues are common, and it appears to be much better and safer to have the conversations out in the open rather than in secret.

All last resort options, including physician-assisted death, make sense only if excellent palliative care is already being provided.

Very little is known about the frequency of other last resort practices in the United States. Data from the Netherlands, where all end-of-life practices are regularly studied, suggest that forgoing life-sustaining therapy and prescribing "opioids in large doses" are each reported to account for approximately 20 percent of deaths, which fits with my clinical experience in the United States. There are no reliable data about the frequency of voluntarily stopping eating and drinking in the United States, although the practice is thought to be rare. In our two hospice programs in Rochester, New York, where VSED is permitted and supported as a last resort, it accounts for less than 1 percent of deaths. Sedation to unconsciousness to treat otherwise intractable physical symptoms appears to be used very variably in the United States, apparently depending more on the values and practice patterns of the practitioners than of the patients. Reports vary from no deaths to half of all deaths, depending in part on definitions but also on practice patterns. At our hospital, where sedation to unconsciousness for treatment of intractable symptoms is subject to guidelines and restrictions that include a mandatory palliative care consult, it accounts for less than 1 percent of deaths.

Physician-Assisted Death in Practice

All last resort options, including physician-assisted death, make sense only if excellent palliative care is already being provided. Mandatory palliative care consultation should therefore be a standard safeguard for any and all of these practices. Over the *next* ten years, medical institutions and professional groups should ensure that all clinicians who care for seriously ill patients are competent in the basics of palliative care and that specialty-based palliative care consultation is available for the more challenging cases.

Some patients will prefer access to physician-assisted death even if the other last resort options are predictably available.

There is also a need to develop explicit, predictable strategies to respond to difficult clinical situations where patients experience severe suffering despite state-of-the-art palliative care. Many of these patients will benefit from a discussion and exploration of last resort options that may or may not include physician-assisted death. There are two main clinical situations in which this might come up:

Patients who are worried about future suffering and wonder what options would be available to them. This conversation begins with an exploration about hopes, fears, and prior experiences of family and friends. Such patients frequently want to know what options they could have in the future if their suffering becomes unacceptable to them. In response to these inquiries, the clinician should talk to the patient about how he or she approaches such situations and what last resort options could be provided if needed. Many patients are reassured by learning about options other than physician-assisted death and by the willingness of the clinician to explore this domain and to commit to working with them and addressing their suffering throughout the illness until death. They can then be free to spend their remaining time and energy on other important personal and family matters.

Patients who eventually experience suffering that is unacceptable to them. This is a much smaller population than those who are worried about the future, but these patients' needs can be more challenging. The starting point is always to explore the patient's suffering in its totality, including why it is now experienced as unacceptable. Part of this assessment is to ensure that standard palliative care is being skillfully applied, and that the request does not emanate from anxiety or depression that might be otherwise addressed. A second opinion by a specialist in palliative care should be obtained. If there are no good alternatives, then the last resort options that are legally available should be explored in the approximate order presented in this paper. Usually, but not always, options other than physician-assisted death will adequately address the patient's clinical situation and be acceptable to the patient. In the event that no other possibilities are workable or acceptable, physician-assisted death would need to be considered in light of the legal environment (the approach in Oregon will be very different than the rest of the country) and the values of patient, family, and clinician.

The Option of Physician-Assisted Death

Some patients will prefer access to physician-assisted death even if the other last resort options are predictably available. Patients who request and eventually act using physician-assisted death in Oregon have a strong interest in controlling their fate, and physician-assisted death puts more choice directly in their hands. However, all the last resort options, including physician-assisted death, are imperfect. Although each addresses some situations particularly well, there are other situations where they would not be as helpful.

Most patients will be reassured by the possibility of an escape, and the vast majority will never need to activate that possibility.

For example, voluntarily stopping eating and drinking has the advantage of putting the decision in the patient's hands, but it requires tremendous discipline not to drink if one is thirsty and capable of drinking, and the duration of the process is too long if symptoms are severe and immediate. On the other hand, medical sedation to unconsciousness may be very frightening to those who value consciousness and being in charge, and there is no way to verify that the sedated patient is not still suffering but unable to report it. Finally, physician-assisted death requires that the patient be physically capable of self-administration and able to swallow a concentrated amount of lethal medication. In addition to these practical issues, any of these options may be morally troubling for patient, family, physician, or staff.

Adding physician-assisted death to the list of last resort options has both risks and benefits. One benefit is that it adds another important possibility for terminally ill patients who experience unacceptable suffering. We should be as responsive as possible to these patients without violating fundamental values, but it is clear that the patient's values in this context count the most, followed by the family and then the clinician (if the course of action requires the physician's participation). Most patients will be reassured by the possibility of an escape, and the vast majority will never need to activate that possibility. But some patients will need a way out, and arbitrarily withholding one important option from patients whose options are so limited seems unfair.

Parents Should Have the Right to Choose Assisted Suicide for Their Children

Jacob M. Appel

Jacob M. Appel, a bioethicist and medical historian, has taught at Brown University and at New York University.

Advocates for aid-in-dying have largely focused their efforts on the rights of mentally-competent adults to end their lives when and how they wish. The two states that have legalized physician-assisted termination via statute, Oregon and Washington, explicitly limit the practice to terminally-ill patients *over the age of eighteen.* Such an emphasis on the suffering of adults is understandable. After all, the illnesses most likely to create a demand for lethal prescriptions, from cancer to ALS [amyotrophic lateral sclerosis, or Lou Gehrig's disease], increase in frequency with age. Unfortunately, much less attention has been paid to efforts to hasten the deaths of pediatric patients who lack any hope of recovery. That is why advocates for children should welcome an impressive study, published this week [March 3, 2010,] in the *Archives of Pediatrics & Adolescent Medicine,* which revealed a considerable interest in euthanasia among the surviving parents of children who had died from cancer. In interviews with 141 such parents, Dr. Veronica Dussel and her colleagues found that greater than 10% considered hastening their children's deaths, and that at least three families believed that physicians had expedited the deaths of their children in direct response to their requests. While the loss of a child to cancer is certainly a tragedy of the greatest magnitude—and one in which it is difficult to imagine finding any silver lining—the courage of these parents in sharing their views with investigators might prove the impetus our society needs to drive pediatric aid-in-dying out of the medical closet. In an era of parental rights and child welfare, maybe we are finally ready to grant suffering minors the right to die.

In an era of parental rights and child welfare, maybe we are finally ready to grant suffering minors the right to die.

The Double-Effect Approach

The medical establishment's longstanding and inadequate solution to the suffering of terminally-ill patients, both children and adults, has been to rely upon the convenient ethical fiction of "double effect." According to the "double effect" principle administering life-shortening medications such as morphine to a patient is permissible if the primary intent is to ease pain—although a faster demise is a likely or inevitable secondary consequence. Thomas Aquinas first proposed this moral sleight-of-hand in the thirteenth century, when defending killings in self defense, and Pope Pius XII overtly endorsed such an approach to medical care in February, 1957. The American Medical Association and the American Academy of Pediatrics, which both oppose so-called active euthanasia, have embraced the doctrine as well. Yet the challenges of relying upon this clever if hazy principle far outweigh the benefits. Needless to say, many physicians will disagree about precisely when pain control ends and aid-in-dying begins—and the result may be that children continue to suffer. Fear of law enforcement drawing this same line in an overly-conservative manner may also scare some well-intentioned oncologists and pediatricians into withholding medication necessary for pain control. Few physicians, no matter how noble and dedicated, are willing to risk a second degree murder charge in order to incrementally reduce the suffering of a patient who will soon expire anyway. Yet even if the "double effect" approach could guarantee that all afflicted children might die without experiencing any physical pain or corporeal discomfort, which is highly implausible, such an approach would do little to staunch the emotional and existential anguish of the patient or her survivors.

One powerful exchange that has been quoted extensively in the media since the appearance of Dussel's study is that between David Reilly, the father of a five-year-old boy who died of cancer in 1999, and his physician, Joanne Wolfe of the Dana-Farber Cancer Institute in Boston. If the child's soft-tissue tumor ever threatened to choke his son to a "horrible, horrible" death, Reilly reportedly asked, "Can we just get it over with quickly?" Wolfe refused. As a result, not only did Reilly endure the loss of his child, but also the solace of knowing that an "out" existed if such suffering ever became intolerable. Yet it is this hypothetical possibility of assistance with dying—as much as any tangible aid—that would provide some meaningful comfort to the parents of many critically-ill children. In the same way that more terminal patients investigate physician-assisted termination in Oregon and the Netherlands than actually use it, the greatest benefit of a legal right to die may stem from the sense of autonomy and empowerment that having such a right grants to individuals who have lost control of almost every other aspect of existence. For the parents of a critically-ill child, such an "escape hatch" might well prove particularly comforting. In contrast, feeling morally compelled to request terminal help that parents know is illegal might further compound their distress.

The Rights of Parents

One of the bedrock tenets of American law is that parents may make medical decisions for their children except in the rare and extreme circumstances where parental wishes and societal notions of child welfare conflict. In the case of young children who cannot understand medical matters, parents are permitted to consent vicariously to their treatment. Our society takes such an approach to pediatric care because—excluding active threats to the public health—we generally believe that parents have a right to raise their offspring as they see fit, and that children are more likely to share the values of their mothers and fathers than those of medical personnel or hospital administrators. So if we are going to carve out an exception to parental authority with regard to end-of-life matters, we would need a compelling reason. Such a justification might exist in the extremely unlikely case where an older child left instructions opposing a hastened death or remained lucid and actively sought extraordinary care, and yet parents sought early termination anyway—a scenario which would clearly raise a compelling argument for overriding parental will. However, if an unconscious, terminally-ill child's views are unknown, or a dying child is simply too young to comprehend death, parents ought to have every right to declare "enough is enough" and to obtain assistance from a physician in bringing a family tragedy to a speedy and decisive conclusion. Moreover, the parents should be allowed to make such a request legally and publicly, without shame or stigma, rather than having to rely on the *sub rosa* [secret] tactics of brave but discreet providers.

In matters of child dying, as in child rearing, an enlightened society should be willing to say that parents know best.

In an ideal world, of course, no children would ever suffer from terminal disease. The cruel reality is that cancer alone kills more than two thousand kids each year in the United States, and thousands of others succumb to chronic genetic disorders, such as cystic fibrosis, or perish in ICU [intensive care unit] beds after sustaining irreversible trauma. These are real children—not hypothetical entities injured for the intellectual benefit of philosophers and theologians. Some opponents of pediatric aid-in-dying argue that legalizing the hastening of death will open the door to exploitation and that a horde of nefarious parents will use this opportunity to rid themselves of burdensome offspring. Strong evidence casts doubt upon these claims, as those jurisdictions that have legalized aid-in-dying for adults have not seen any such abuse of the elderly or disabled. Similarly, if the fear is that insurance companies and corporate hospitals will pressure families into terminating care prematurely—which they are just as likely to do in a world governed by the willful self-deception of "double effect"—then the proper solution is to curtail the power of hospital and health insurers, not to force unwanted life of minimal quality on our most vulnerable citizens.

Granting parents the right to hasten the deaths of their dying children certainty does not prevent either physicians or the courts from intervening in the unlikely event that a caregiver appears to be guided by base and ulterior motives. What establishing such a right does ensure is that children and parents will have one more weapon in their arsenal when confronting the tragedy of fatal illness. If I had a young child who had no prospect of regaining consciousness, I would want her existence ended as quickly and painlessly as possible. That is not to suggest that other reasonable people might choose differently. Up to the point that the public welfare is gravely compromised, those families who wish to keep comatose children alive should certainly be permitted to do so. In matters of child dying, as in child rearing, an enlightened society should be willing to say that parents know best.

There Is No Justification for Legalizing Euthanasia

Peter C. Glover

Peter C. Glover is a British writer specializing in politics, the media, and cultural affairs.

The courts in the English-speaking world have recently witnessed a number of high-profile and distressing cases where individuals have argued both for the 'right to die' and even the 'right to live' in the event of incapacitation. But it was perhaps in the troubling case of the young American woman Terri Schiavo that the issues surrounding euthanasia have been most hotly debated. This was a case that, like no other, split the conscience of a nation, causing a public debate which cut deep into the American psyche and exposed the core ethical arguments surrounding the whole morality of euthanasia or assisted suicide as never before.

At the heart of the debate was not only the 'human right' to choose death, but the 'right' for society, in general, to be complicit in its acquiescence, hence *legally*.

The Terminology of Suicide and Euthanasia

Before we get to grips with the issue itself, however, it is important, if we wish to avoid the confusion that often derails genuine debate, to clarify our terminology.

1. *Suicide*—is self-killing, some would say self-murder.

2. *Assisted suicide*—involves enlisting the aid of another person, often a doctor, to end one's own life. Those 'assisting' provide *the means* of death but do not take part in the killing directly.

Peter C. Glover, "Euthanasia: Can It Ever Be Right to Legalise It?," *Catholic Insight*, vol. 17, no. 2, February 2009, pp. 8–9. All rights reserved. Reproduced by permission.

3. *Euthanasia*—occurs when someone other than the 'patient'—a doctor, nurse or someone else—performs an action, such as a lethal injection, which brings about death.

4. *Passive euthanasia*—occurs when the withdrawal of medical assistance or life-sustaining treatment leads 'naturally' to the death of the patient. This term is seldom used because of the near universal agreement that it is, and has always been, a justifiable treatment ethically (i.e. allowing 'nature' to take its course).

Let me state my case here bluntly: with the exception of no. 4, which has been largely unquestioned common medical practice for centuries, none of the other three (suicide, assisted suicide or euthanasia) has any moral justification in the light of sound reason and/or medical science.

The Judeo-Christian worldview is a well-reasoned pattern of belief in which the sanctity of life is given moral substance.

I am opposed to euthanasia in all its forms, not just because I, as a Christian, believe the Creator God is *demonstrably* opposed to it, making no provision for it in His revealed will to mankind and through the teaching of the Catholic Church, but also because the biblical and Church teaching, which is *not* the subject of this particular article, is wholly supported by every ethical, philosophical and reasoned argument available. I mention my biblical worldview here with good reason. All too often, the issue of worldview is obscured in the public debate. Indeed, many Christians even feel it judicious not to mention it at all, as if the assumption is that the secular person, unlike the Christian, does not possess a 'worldview' or cultural or philosophical spectacles through which he views the world. Nothing could be further from the truth! It is just a case of articulating what one's worldview is, and how it affects and underpins the views or opinions being expressed.

This is no secondary matter whenever any moral issue is being discussed. When all is said and done, the Judeo-Christian worldview is a well-reasoned pattern of belief in which the sanctity of life is given moral substance. Those who criticise such a worldview ought to be called upon to articulate and uphold their own.

The Moral Gold Standard

The advantage here is that we can point to a 'gold standard' of moral right or wrong—in fact *the* moral gold standard which is the foundation of Western civilization's Judeo-Christian heritage. Those who hold secular and liberal privatised worldviews often struggle to sustain them. While the biblical and conservative worldview is focused on the higher good of the community, one usually finds that the secular liberal focuses on the rights of the individual. The reality is, however, that one must outweigh the other. And the Bible as well as historic tradition dictates that it must be the higher good of the community that wins out.

Having made this important point, however, in this article I intend to equip the ordinary Catholic Christian with insight into the case against the legalisation of euthanasia from a secular perspective to reinforce the biblical argument.

The more difficult but humane solution to human suffering is to address the problem, not get rid of the human.

Here, in a nutshell, are the very practical and key arguments *against* legalising euthanasia/assisted suicide *in any form*:

1. *A request for assisted suicide is typically a cry for help.* In reality it is typically a call for counselling, assistance and positive alternatives as solutions to very *real* problems.

2. *Suicidal intent is typically transient.* Of those who attempt suicide, fewer than 4% go on to kill themselves in the next five years; less than 11% will commit suicide over the next 35 years.

3. *Terminally ill patients who desire death are typically depressed—and depression is treatable.* In one study, 24% of those desiring death had clinical depression.

4. *Pain is controllable.* The array of treatments to control pain (palliative care) is vast and impressive today. Often the person seeking death does not need assistance to commit suicide but a doctor *better trained* in palliative care. The Nightingale Alliance states that 95% of all pain is controllable and the other 5% can be reduced to a tolerable level.

5. *Legalising voluntary euthanasia almost always means legalising non-voluntary euthanasia.* In America, for instance, state courts have consistently ruled that if competent people have a right, then *incompetent* people must be 'given' the same 'right.' It is highly likely that the British courts would rule the same way.

6. *The Netherlands' experience in legalising voluntary assisted suicide for those with terminal illness has spread to include non-voluntary euthanasia for people with no terminal illness.* Half of the killings in the Netherlands are now non-voluntary and a 'culture of death,' admitted as such privately by many Dutch doctors, has now taken root there. It has become a common legal 'solution' for those with mental illness, permanent disability, and even old age.

7. *You don't solve problems by getting rid of the people to whom the problems happen.* The more difficult but humane solution to human suffering is to address the problem, not get rid of the human. . . .

No Justification for Legal Suicide

[There] are no scientific, medical or ethical reasons why any of us, not just Catholic Christians, should condone or support the legalisation of euthanasia in society.

No one can prevent someone, intent on the act, from taking out a revolver and blowing his brains out, or administering a lethal dose of drugs to himself or another. But that is *not* the issue here.

The issue here is whether there are sound reasons why a society and a nation should acquiesce in *the process* by legalising it. If we are intent on protecting the weak and retaining our current culture of life, in the Hippocratic tradition, then we must face whether we would rather introduce a culture of uncertainty and of death as has happened in the Netherlands. A culture where we can never be sure whether someone, somewhere, believes that our 'quality of life' is such that the world—according to *their* worldview—would be better off without us or those we love, brings dreadful uncertainty and immense unnecessary suffering.

Euthanasia and Assisted Suicide Should Not Be Legal

Rita L. Marker and Kathi Hamlon

Rita L. Marker is executive director and Kathi Hamlon is policy analyst of the Patients Rights Council, previously known as the International Task Force on Euthanasia and Assisted Suicide.

One of the most important public policy debates today surrounds the issues of euthanasia and assisted suicide. The outcome of that debate will profoundly affect family relationships, interaction between doctors and patients, and concepts of basic ethical behavior. With so much at stake, more is needed than a duel of one-liners, slogans and sound bites.

The following answers to frequently asked questions are designed as starting points for considering the issues. . . .

Legal Euthanasia and Assisted Suicide

What is the difference between euthanasia and assisted suicide?

One way to distinguish them is to look at the last act—the act without which death would not occur.

Using this distinction, if a third party performs the last act that intentionally causes a patient's death, euthanasia has occurred. For example, giving a patient a lethal injection or putting a plastic bag over her head to suffocate her would be considered euthanasia.

On the other hand, if the person who dies performs the last act, assisted suicide has taken place. Thus it would be assisted suicide if a person swallows an overdose of drugs that has been provided by a doctor for the purpose of causing death. It would also be assisted suicide if a patient pushes a

Rita L. Marker and Kathi Hamlon, "Euthanasia and Assisted Suicide: Frequently Asked Questions," Patients Rights Council, January 2010. All rights reserved. Reproduced by permission.

switch to trigger a fatal injection after the doctor has inserted an intravenous needle into the patient's vein. . . .

The Role of the Law

Should people be forced to stay alive?

No. A lot of people think that euthanasia or assisted suicide is needed so patients won't be forced to remain alive by being "hooked up" to machines. But the law already permits patients or their surrogates to withhold or withdraw unwanted medical treatment even if that increases the likelihood that the patient will die. Thus, no one needs to be hooked up to machines against their will.

Neither the law nor medical ethics requires that "everything be done" to keep a person alive. Insistence, against the patient's wishes, that death be postponed by every means available is contrary to law and practice. It is also cruel and inhumane.

There comes a time when continued attempts to cure are not compassionate, wise, or medically sound. That's when hospice, including in-home hospice care, can be of great help. That is the time when all efforts should be directed to making the patient's remaining time comfortable. Then, all interventions should be directed to alleviating pain and other symptoms as well as to providing emotional and spiritual support for both the patient and the patient's loved ones.

Laws against euthanasia and assisted suicide are in place to prevent abuse and to protect people from unscrupulous doctors and others.

Does the government have the right to make people suffer?

Absolutely not. Likewise, the government should not have the right to give one group of people (e.g. doctors) the power to kill another group of people (e.g. their patients).

Activists often claim that laws against euthanasia and assisted suicide are government mandated suffering. But this claim would be similar to saying that laws against selling contaminated food are government mandated starvation.

Laws against euthanasia and assisted suicide are in place to prevent abuse and to protect people from unscrupulous doctors and others. They are not, and never have been, intended to make anyone suffer.

Suicide and Killing

But shouldn't people have the right to commit suicide?

People do have the power to commit suicide. Worldwide, about a million people commit suicide annually. Suicide and attempted suicide are not criminalized. Each and every year, in the United States alone, there are 1.6 times as many suicides as there are homicides. And, internationally, suicide is one of the three leading causes of death among people ages 15–34.

Suicide is an all too common tragic, individual act. Indeed, in 1999, the Surgeon General of the United States launched a campaign to reduce the rate of suicide.

Euthanasia and assisted suicide are not private acts. Rather, they involve one person facilitating the death of another. This is a matter of very public concern since it can lead to tremendous abuse, exploitation and erosion of care for the most vulnerable people among us.

Euthanasia and assisted suicide are not about giving rights to the person who dies but, instead, they are about changing public policy so that doctors or others can directly and intentionally end or participate in ending another person's life. Euthanasia and assisted suicide are not about the right to die. They are about the right to kill.

Isn't "kill" too strong a word for euthanasia and assisted suicide?

No. The word "kill" means "to cause the death of."

In 1989, a group of physicians published a report in the *New England Journal of Medicine* in which they concluded that it would be morally acceptable for doctors to give patients suicide information and a prescription for deadly drugs so they can kill themselves. Dr. Ronald Cranford, one of the authors of the report, publicly acknowledged that this was "the same as killing the patient."

While changes in laws have transformed euthanasia and/or assisted suicide from crimes into "medical treatments" in Oregon, Washington, Belgium, Luxembourg, and the Netherlands, the reality has not changed—patients are being killed.

Proponents of euthanasia and assisted suicide often use euphemisms like "deliverance," "death with dignity," "aid-in-dying" and "gentle landing." If a proposed change in public policy has to be promoted with euphemisms, this may be due to the fact that the use of accurate, descriptive language would make its chilling reality too obvious.

The Terminally Ill

Wouldn't euthanasia or assisted suicide only be available to people who are terminally ill?

No. There are two problems here—the definition of "terminal" and the changes that have already taken place to extend euthanasia or assisted suicide to those who aren't "terminally ill."

> *If euthanasia is legal, a court challenge could result in a finding that a surrogate could make a request for death on behalf of a child or an adult who doesn't have decision-making capacity.*

There are many definitions for the word "terminal." For example, Jack Kevorkian who participated in the deaths of more than 130 people before he was convicted of murder said that a terminal illness was "any disease that curtails life even for a day." Dutch psychiatrist Dr. Boudewijn Chabot who provided a fatal dose of drugs to a depressed, but physically healthy, woman, stated that "persistently suicidal patients are, indeed, terminal."

Oregon's and Washington's assisted-suicide laws define "terminal" as a condition which will "within reasonable medical judgment, produce death within six months." A prognosis of six month to live is also the basis upon which patients qualify for hospice coverage under Medicare. However, federal officials note that about 10% of patients live longer than the anticipated six-month life expectancy. . . .

The idea that euthanasia and assisted suicide should only be practiced if a patient has a terminal condition has never been accepted in the Netherlands. Under both the previous guidelines and the new law in the Netherlands, unbearable suffering of either a physical or mental nature has been the factor that qualifies one for induced death.

It appears that not even the prerequisite of subjective unbearable suffering will be maintained for much longer. Discussion now centers on whether assisted suicide should be available to elderly people who are healthy but "tired of life." Dutch Minister of Justice Els Borst has said, "I am not against it if it can be carefully controlled so that only those people of advanced age who are tired of life can use it."

Assisted suicide for non-terminally ill patients has also been advocated repeatedly in the United States. . . .

The Risk of Pressure to Die

Wouldn't euthanasia and assisted suicide only be at a patient's request?

No. As one of their major goals, euthanasia proponents seek to have euthanasia and assisted suicide considered "medical treatment." If one accepts the notion that euthanasia or assisted suicide is a good medical treatment, then it would not only be inappropriate, but discriminatory, to deny this good treatment to a person solely because that person is too young or mentally incapacitated to request it.

In the United States, a surrogate's decision is often treated, for legal purposes, as if the patient had made it. That means that, if euthanasia is legal, a court challenge could result in a finding that a surrogate could make a request for death on behalf of a child or an adult who doesn't have decision-making capacity.

In the Netherlands, a 1990 government sponsored survey found that .8% of all deaths in the Netherlands were euthanasia deaths that occurred without a request from the patient. And in a 1995 study, Dutch doctors reported ending the lives of 948 patients without their request.

Suppose, however that surrogates were not permitted to choose death for another and that doctors did not end patients' lives without their request. The fact still remains that subtle, even unintended, pressure would still be unavoidable.

A Case in Point

Such was the case with an elderly woman who died under Oregon's assisted suicide law [as reported by Erin Barnett]:

Kate Cheney, 85, reportedly had been suffering from early dementia. After she was diagnosed with cancer, her own physician declined to provide a lethal prescription for her. Counseling was sought to determine if she was capable of making health care decisions.

A psychiatrist found that Mrs. Cheney was not eligible for assisted suicide since she was not explicitly pushing for it, her daughter seemed to be coaching her to do so, and she couldn't remember important names and details of even a recent hospital stay.

Mrs. Cheney was then taken to a psychologist who said she was competent but possibly under the influence of her daughter who was "somewhat coercive." Finally, a managed care ethicist who was overseeing her case determined that she was qualified for assisted suicide, and the lethal drugs were prescribed.

Could euthanasia or assisted suicide be used as a means of health care cost containment?

Yes. Perhaps one of the most important developments in recent years is the increasing emphasis placed on health care providers to contain costs. In such a climate, euthanasia or assisted suicide certainly could become a means of cost containment.

These implications were acknowledged during a historic argument before the U.S. Supreme Court. Arguing against assisted suicide, acting solicitor general Walter Dellinger said, "The least costly treatment for any illness is lethal medication."

Legalized euthanasia or assisted suicide raises the potential for a profoundly dangerous situation in which the "choice" of assisted suicide or euthanasia is the only affordable option for some people.

In the United States alone, millions of people have no medical insurance and studies have shown that the elderly, the poor and minorities are often denied access to needed treatment or pain control. Doctors are being pressured by HMOs [health maintenance organizations] to reduce care; "futile care guidelines" are being instituted, enabling health facilities to deny necessary and wanted interventions; and health care providers are often likely to benefit financially from providing less, rather than more, care for their patients.

In Oregon, some patients have been told by their health insurance provider that a costly drug prescribed by a doctor to treat the patient's illness would not be covered but inexpensive lethal drugs for assisted suicide would be.

Canadians are faced with such long delays getting treatment in the country's overcrowded health care system that the Canadian government has contracted for Canadians to be treated out of the country.

Many British doctors and nurses have concluded that the only way to secure the future of the National Health Service (NHS) is to make more treatments available only to those who can pay privately for them. And a survey by the Nuffield Trust and the nurses' magazine, *Nursing Times*, found that the NHS is failing to care adequately for hundreds of thousands of patients who die each year, many without proper care or pain relief.

The debate over euthanasia and assisted suicide is about public policy and the law.

Savings to governments could become a consideration. Drugs for assisted suicide cost about $75 to $100, making them far less expensive than providing medical care. This could fill the void from cutbacks for treatment and care with the "treatment" of death.

For example, the Oregon Medicaid program pays for assisted suicide for poor residents as a means of "comfort care." In addition, spokespersons for non-governmental health insurance plans have said the coverage of assisted suicide is "no different than any other covered prescription."

Legalized euthanasia or assisted suicide raises the potential for a profoundly dangerous situation in which the "choice" of assisted suicide or euthanasia is the only affordable option for some people. . . .

The Law and Religion

Isn't opposition to euthanasia and assisted suicide just an attempt to impose religious beliefs on others?

No. Right-to-die leaders have attempted for a long time to make it seem that anyone against euthanasia or assisted suicide is trying to impose his or her religion on others. But that's not the case.

People on both sides of the euthanasia and assisted suicide controversies claim membership in religious denominations. There are also individuals on both sides who claim no religious affiliation at all. But it's even more important to realize that these are not religious issues, nor should this be a religious debate.

The debate over euthanasia and assisted suicide is about public policy and the law.

With legalized euthanasia or assisted suicide, condemned killers would have more rights to have their lives protected than would vulnerable people who could be pressured and exploited into what amounts to capital punishment for the "crime" of being sick, old, disabled or dependent.

The fact that the religious convictions of some people parallel what has been long-standing public policy does not disqualify them from taking a stand on an issue.

For example, there are laws that prohibit sales clerks from stealing company profits. Although these laws coincide with religious beliefs, it would be absurd to suggest that such laws should be eliminated. And it would be equally ridiculous to say that a person who has religious opposition to it shouldn't be able to support laws against stealing.

Similarly, the fact that the religious convictions of some euthanasia and assisted-suicide opponents parallel what has been long-standing public policy does not disqualify them from taking a stand on the issues.

Throughout all of modern history, laws have prohibited mercy killing. The need for such laws has been, and should continue to be, debated on the basis of public policy. And people of any or no religious belief should have the right to be involved in that debate.

In Washington state, where an attempt to legalize euthanasia and assisted suicide by voter initiative in 1991 failed, polls taken within days of the vote indicated that fewer than ten percent of those who opposed the measure had done so for religious reasons.

Voter initiatives have also failed in California, Michigan and Maine. All failed following significant organized opposition from a coalition of groups including medical societies, nursing groups, hospice associations, civil rights groups and major state newspapers. . . .

The Importance of Legal Prohibition

Since suicide isn't against the law, why should it be illegal to help someone commit suicide?

Neither suicide nor attempted suicide is criminalized anywhere in the United States or in many other countries. This is not because of any "right" to suicide. When penalties against attempted suicide were removed, legal scholars made it clear that this was not done for the purpose of permitting suicide. Instead it was intended to prevent suicide. Penalties were removed so people could seek help in dealing with the problems they're facing without risk of being prosecuted if it were discovered that they had attempted suicide.

Just as current public policy does not grant a "right" to be killed to a person who is suicidal because of a lost business, neither should it permit people to be killed because they are in despair over their physical or emotional condition. With legalized euthanasia or assisted suicide, condemned killers would have more rights to have their lives protected than would vulnerable people who could be pressured and exploited into what amounts to capital punishment for the "crime" of being sick, old, disabled or dependent.

The Euthanasia of Children Should Not Be Allowed

Wesley J. Smith

Wesley J. Smith is a senior fellow in human rights and bioethics at the Discovery Institute, a legal consultant to the Patients Rights Council, and a special consultant for the Center for Bioethics and Culture. He is the author of Forced Exit: Euthanasia, Assisted Suicide and the New Duty to Die.

The push to permit infanticide has entered the mainstream. The Royal College of Obstetricians and Gynaecologists (RCOG) has recommended that a debate be had about whether to permit "deliberate interventions to kill infants." The recommendation, which was widely reported in the media, was in response to a query from the Nuffield Council on Bioethics concerning ethical issues pertaining to health care which prolongs the life of newborns. It was at the urging of the RCOG that euthanasia of infants was added to the topics that the council would consider. As reported by the London *Times*, the RCOG's recommendation states:

> A very disabled child can mean a disabled family. If life-shortening and deliberate interventions to kill infants were available, they might have an impact on obstetric decision-making, even preventing some late term abortions, as some parents would be more confident about continuing a pregnancy and taking a risk on outcome.

The article goes on to quote a number of British doctors and professors who support euthanasia.

Consider carefully what has happened here. A prestigious medical association has seriously suggested that killing some babies because they are seriously ill or disabled might be ethically acceptable and, at the very least, is worthy of considered and respectable debate. It is about time that people start paying attention to this. Those who think that legal infanticide is unthinkable and preposterous are being naïve. Infanticide advocacy is no longer limited to rogue bioethicists, such as Princeton University's notorious Peter Singer, who has famously argued that parents be given as much as a year to decide whether to keep or kill their babies.

In fact, it has been some time since Singer was the dominant voice of infanticide advocacy. In recent years, articles aimed at normalizing the killing of disabled babies have appeared in some of the world's most established medical publications. For example, the March 10, 2005, edition of the *New England Journal of Medicine* [*NEJM*] published an article by Dutch physicians who have admitted to having euthanized 15–20 disabled infants. The *NEJM* provided them with a respectable forum in which to propose formal regulations to govern what amounts to eugenic infanticide. The so-called "Groningen Protocol" (named after the Dutch hospital where the infanticides took place) posits three categories of killable infants: babies "with no chance of survival"; infants with a "poor prognosis and [who] are dependent on intensive care"; and "infants with a hopeless prognosis," including those "not depending on intensive medical treatment but for whom a very poor quality of life . . . is predicted."

The Issue of Suffering

Such journal articles were reported on approvingly in the mainstream media. For example, the July 10, 2005, *New York Times Magazine* published a column by frequent contributor Jim Holt proposing the merits of the Groningen Protocol. Holt suggested that the decision to kill ill or disabled babies should be governed by "a new moral duty," namely, "the duty prevent suffering, especially futile suffering."

The debate over infant euthanasia is usually framed as a collision between two values: sanctity of life and quality of life. Judgments about the latter, of course, are notoriously subjective and can lead you down a slippery slope. But shifting the emphasis to suffering changes the terms of the debate. To keep alive an infant whose short life expectancy will be dominated by pain—pain that it can neither bear nor comprehend—is, it might be argued, to do that infant a continuous injury.

At first blush, this might seem reasonable, but Holt's game of semantics does not provide him with traction on the slippery slope. The concept of suffering is not limited to pain, but must also take account of "quality of life," as more liberal advocates of infanticide would surely point out. More insidiously, Holt's advocacy could lead to a perceived duty to kill disabled babies since he argues that not killing a disabled baby could be to inflict injury upon the child.

History shows that this is how baby killing begins—by convincing ourselves that there is such a thing as a human life not worth living, and hence, not worth protecting.

Such arguments are really a veneer for the real issues, which are money and commitment. Disabled infants are expensive to care for, particularly if they don't die young, and they require all sorts of attention. The nub of the issue isn't about our supposed inability to alleviate the suffering of infants—a false supposition—but rather, about our not wanting to spend the financial and emotional resources it would take to do so. This position is clearly central to the RCOG's statement—and was explicitly ratified in a November 9, 2006, editorial in *The Economist* calling the RCOG's call to debate infanticide "brave" and urging that infanticide be seriously considered because "Disabled children are nine times more likely than others to end up in the care of the state."

Infanticide, alas, has become a respectable notion, at least among some elite opinion makers. History shows that this is how baby killing begins—by convincing ourselves that there is such a thing as a human life not worth living, and hence, not worth protecting. By calling for a serious debate about infanticide, the RCOG has badly subverted the foundational moral principle that each and every human being has equal moral value simply and merely because he or she is human.

CHAPTER 2

Is Assisted Suicide Moral?

Overview: Americans' Views on the Morality of Assisted Suicide

Joseph Carroll

Joseph Carroll is an assistant editor for Gallup, an international polling, news, research, and consultancy organization.

Jack Kevorkian, the Michigan doctor who assisted more than 130 terminally ill patients with ending their life, will be released from prison on parole this Friday [June 1, 2007]: Gallup's annual Values and Beliefs poll finds Americans are generally divided about whether doctor-assisted suicide is morally acceptable or morally wrong. Even so, a majority of Americans believe doctors should be allowed to help a terminally ill patient commit "suicide" if the patient requests it. Most Americans also say doctors should be allowed by law to "end" a terminally ill patient's life by some painless means if the patient and family request it. Republicans are more likely than Democrats to oppose these right-to-die issues, as are frequent churchgoers compared with those who rarely or never attend church.

According to the May 10–13, 2007 poll, 49% of Americans say doctor-assisted suicide is morally acceptable, while 44% say it is morally wrong. Americans have been closely divided about the moral acceptability of doctor-assisted suicide since this specific morality question was first asked in 2001. The percentage of Americans saying assisted suicide is morally acceptable has averaged 49%, with a low of 45% and a high of 53%.

Of the 16 issues tested in the poll for moral acceptability, doctor-assisted suicide ranks in the middle of the list, scoring similarly to gay and lesbian relations. Americans are most likely to say the death penalty, divorce, stem cell research, and gambling are morally acceptable, with at least 6 in 10 describing each of these issues as morally acceptable. Americans are least likely to view adultery, polygamy, human cloning, and suicide as acceptable.

Public Opinion on the Legal Issue

A majority of Americans in the poll support both euthanasia and doctor-assisted suicide.

Half of the respondents in the survey were asked about doctor-assisted suicide using the following wording:

> "When a person has a disease that cannot be cured and is living in severe pain, do you think doctors should or should not be allowed by law to assist the patient to commit suicide if the patient requests it?"

The results show that 56% of Americans support this and 38% do not.

Gallup has asked a more general question regarding the acceptance of physicians assisting in ending suffering patients' lives since 1996—when the term "doctor-assisted suicide" started to come into use in the news coverage of Kevorkian. A majority have always supported doctor-assisted suicide, with a high point of 68% support in 2001. The current 56% level of support is on the low end for what Gallup has found.

The other half of the respondents in the survey were asked about euthanasia more generally:

> "When a person has a disease that cannot be cured, do you think doctors should be allowed by law to end the patient's life by some painless means if the patient and his or her family request it?"

Support for euthanasia has always been higher than support for doctor-assisted suicide. In the current poll, 71% favor euthanasia, while 27% oppose it.

Over time, support for euthanasia has increased substantially. When this question was first asked in 1947 and again in 1950, only about one in three Americans said they supported euthanasia. Support reached the majority level in 1973, with 53% supporting it. Since 1990, support has been much higher, ranging from 65% to 75%.

Fifty-nine percent of Democrats believe doctor-assisted suicide is morally acceptable. A similar percentage of Republicans, 54%, feel it is morally wrong.

Democrats (including independents who lean toward the Democratic Party) are much more likely than Republicans (including Republican-leaning independents) to support euthanasia and doctor-assisted suicide.

Seventy-seven percent of Democrats say doctors should be allowed to end a terminally ill patient's life by some painless means if the patient and family request it. Among Republicans, 64% support this notion.

When it comes to doctors assisting a terminally ill patient to commit suicide, 62% of Democrats and only 49% of Republicans support this.

Fifty-nine percent of Democrats believe doctor-assisted suicide is morally acceptable. A similar percentage of Republicans, 54%, feel it is morally wrong.

Fewer than half of Americans who attend church services every week support either doctor-assisted suicide or euthanasia, and only 23% of weekly churchgoers say doctor-assisted suicide is morally acceptable. Americans who attend church services less often are much more likely to support the right-to-die issues.

It Is Compassionate to Permit Assisted Suicide

A.C. Grayling

A.C. Grayling is a philosopher and founder of the New College of the Humanities, a private undergraduate college in London.

Controversy always follows those who suggest that terminally ill or incurably suffering people should be allowed to ask for and receive help to die if they so wish. The same set of arguments is standardly urged in opposition: that life is sacred, that legalising physician-assisted suicide would lead to abuses, that a majority of the medical profession do not approve of legalising voluntary euthanasia.

These arguments so far carry the day with our [British] legislators, even though polling shows now, and has done so consistently for many years, that more than 80 per cent of the public want physician-assisted suicide to be available to them as an option if they should find themselves in circumstances where their lives have become unbearable without hope of remedy.

The motive behind efforts made by those such as Lord Joffe, Patricia Hewitt, Baroness Warnock and the organisation Dignity in Dying to have physician-assisted suicide legalised is a simple one: it is a humane impulse of kindness, based on the realisation that we are gentler to our pets than to our fellow humans in facilitating an ultimate release from suffering when it is needed. In the case of our fellow humans we are talking about a release from suffering that the sufferers themselves earnestly desire and request; refusing them denies their autonomy, and is at least unkind and at worst cruel.

The spectacle of sufferers having to go to Switzerland to get the easeful death they want, instead of being able to leave life in their own homes, with their family and friends around them and at a time of their own choosing, is a scandal. A civilised and mature society should allow the few—they will always be a very small minority—who desire this option to be granted the right to take it; the coercive paternalism that denies it is wholly unjustified.

The Arguments Against Assisted Suicide

Those who talk of the "sanctity of life" make a fundamental mistake: it is not mere quantity of life that matters, but its quality; and since dying is a living act, the quality of experience at the end of life, or in conditions of incurable distress, is the overriding consideration. To believe that mere length of existence, however unbearable and painful, trumps the kindness of granting someone's request for help to end their suffering easily and quickly, is to have one's priorities utterly wrong.

The argument about the possible abuse of legalised physician-assisted suicide turns mainly on the fear that ill or elderly people might be coerced into it against their wishes by unscrupulous relatives. Alas, abuse is possible in all walks of life, but a carefully drafted law, such as the one Lord Joffe introduced in the House of Lords, would provide careful protections and checks, while allowing those in unbearable distress the sanctuary of an easeful end to suffering.

Polling data about medical attitudes to physician-assisted suicide suggest a third of doctors in favour and two thirds against. Two somewhat inconsistent reasons are offered: the first, that the primary aims of medical practice are curing or at least palliating, never killing; and second, that practitioners already help patients to die but would prefer the grey area of unspoken discretion to remain, fearing that a definite law would make matters more rather than less difficult.

A solution to the large difference between what the public want and what the medical profession wants is to have a medical specialism devoted to assisted dying, either a subsidiary part of anaesthetics or of terminal palliative care. If each NHS [National Health Service] trust had one or two consultants in this specialty, who would help patients who had formally requested assistance to die and been granted it by the Trust ethics committee, all the rest of the staff would be exempt from the obligation, and for them the dilemma—which must frequently enough arise now, but without benefit of legal guidance—would not arise.

To believe that mere length of existence, however unbearable and painful, trumps the kindness of granting someone's request for help to end their suffering easily and quickly, is to have one's priorities utterly wrong.

It is important to emphasise two things. The first is that the option of having help to die when in an unbearable and irremediable situation—suffering pain, suffocation because of inability to swallow, the indignity of incontinence, utter helplessness, reliance on selfhood-diminishing drugs, and the like—and when one has requested that help while mentally competent and with a settled resolution, is a human right that ought to be respected.

The second is that very few of us will ever ask for help to die, because most of us will prefer to live as long as possible, and to fight the diseases and incapacities that come with age. Physician-assisted suicide, if made law along the lines of Lord Joffe's bill, will require a settled determination by the sufferer, properly checked and verified.

Much misinformation is put out about the situation in the Netherlands, where granted requests for physician-assisted death result in less than 0.8 per cent of all deaths annually, mainly in terminally ill or permanently and unbearably disabled people under 66 (thus rebutting the "coerced elderly" concern). More than 90 per cent of these assisted deaths shorten life by less than a month—indeed most of them by less than a week. The number of physician-assisted deaths in the Netherlands has decreased since it was first made legal, and has stabilised at a very low level.

A Continuing Debate

In Britain, to achieve a dignified and chosen end to one's sufferings requires the trouble, difficulty and expense of going to Switzerland. Patricia Hewitt wished to make that task, in the absence of a humane and civilised law in our own country, easier for all concerned. It is a kindly gesture, and a generous one, which I think puts to shame the minority in our country who stand in the way of a mature approach to individual rights over how we end our lives.

One hopes that the debate, ill-informed and retrogressive as much of it is, will continue, and eventually enable the majority opinion to prevail, thus ending unnecessary suffering, and allowing those who so choose to die in dignity and peace.

It Is Merciful to Help a Terminally Ill Person Die

Margery Fridstein

Margery Fridstein is a psychological counselor in Highlands Ranch, Colorado.

In the 1990s, Dr. Jack Kevorkian drew national attention as a right-to-die activist. His career of physician-assisted suicide for terminally ill patients ended for him with a charge of second-degree murder and a prison sentence.

I, like many others, closely followed his story and wondered why there was not more support for him and his wish to help terminally ill people die with dignity. His belief: "Dying is not a crime."

I now believe that as a society, we tend to mistreat terminally ill patients.

My 93-year-old friend Jean is an example. After deciding not to undergo further treatment for her recurring cancer, she could have died with dignity—if only someone could have assisted her death rather than let her wait, month after month, for her body to deteriorate enough for her to die.

By the time my healthy husband contracted a deadly bacterial infection a year later, I had learned enough about dying to help make the right decision for him.

Many people don't have the chance to make a decision at all. Either they haven't prepared themselves, or their doctor or family members influence them otherwise.

Sadly, many doctors seem to consider death a curable disease.

What makes all this even more difficult is that one's own doctor, who has an understanding of and a relationship with

Margery Fridstein, "Lessons in Dying: What Is Wrong with Giving Up When Our Bodies Give Out?," *Denver Post*, November 28, 2010. All rights reserved. Reproduced by permission.

his patient, takes a back seat, while a complete stranger, a hospitalist [a physician who cares for hospitalized patients], attends the critically ill person.

In the Aug. 2 issue of *The New Yorker*, Atul Gawande wrote, "We pay doctors to give chemotherapy and do surgery, but not to take the time required to sort out when doing so is unwise."

The Desire to Die

In the fall of 2008, Jean asked me to help her figure out how to die.

One of her sons had moved her from Aspen to Boulder so he and his wife could watch over her while she waited to die.

She confessed that she had collected 50 sleeping pills, but was fearful of taking them.

"Marge, I had no idea it would be so hard," Jean told me on the phone. "I've been saving pills for this, but now I'm afraid they won't work. You know, when you live to 93, you have a strong heart, and it isn't easy for it to stop."

Jean, a widow for 20 years, was a remarkable woman; strong, bright, clear-headed. She had been well able to take care of herself until a few months before. The uterine cancer that she had beaten at 86 had returned.

Her long-time Aspen doctor, in whom she had great confidence, discussed the options with her. Chemotherapy was likely to give her time, but no cure.

She consulted with an oncologist, her three sons, her friends. She decided that she had lived a wonderful, fulfilling life and that it was time for it to end. She turned her care over to hospice, moved to Boulder and prepared for death.

Luckily, Jean was in no pain and took no medication. Her only symptoms were weakness and fatigue.

Six months went by. The hospice nurse visited her once a week. But she was alone most of the time because her son and his wife worked. Her friends from her old life called and a few tried to travel to see her. But by and large she was very lonely, wishing she could end her life but afraid.

I did what I could to help her, gathering information and ultimately urging her to call Compassion & Choices, a national organization dedicated to the care and rights of terminally ill patients.

A study . . . in 2002 showed that 6 percent of 5,000 physicians interviewed admitted helping their terminal patients die.

A counselor at the Denver office spoke with her and agreed to send some literature. Jean called me when it arrived.

"Marge, I can't read the material," she told me. "I want you to help me. I can't do it myself."

I replied, "Jean, it's quite clear that they do not want me to do anything for you. You have to get the information and make the decisions."

"I can't do it, Marge," Jean lamented.

Washington and Oregon are the only states that allow euthanasia, but there are strict rules as to who qualifies. However, many doctors will recommend palliative sedation to relieve pain.

According to Roland Halpern of Compassion & Choices, a study conducted by *Medical Economics Magazine* in 2002 showed that 6 percent of 5,000 physicians interviewed admitted helping their terminal patients die. It is widely suspected that more doctors do so, but do not admit to it.

Compassion & Choices receives about 250 calls a month for information on end-of-life issues.

A Friend's Death

Each time I saw Jean after that, she was more fragile. She greeted me dressed, sitting alone on her sofa. Her mind was clear but she was so lonely. Once I took her to a neighborhood restaurant for pizza. She ate little.

And then the end came. "Marge, I'm different. You won't recognize me." It had been 2 1/2 weeks since I last visited her, and a caretaker had been hired because she could no longer be alone.

I called Friday to ask about a visit the next day and heard a different Jean. "No, I can't go out to lunch. Marge, this is bad."

I had to answer, "Jean, this is what you have been waiting for." Her soft reply was, "Yes."

When I arrived the next day, her son greeted me. "This is her first really bad day," he said. "She's in her room."

She was in bed, her head propped up with pillows. The oxygen was clicking away. "Oh, Marge, it's bad." She was in pain and had just taken her first dose of morphine. "I had planned for us to visit in the garden, but then this happened."

I kissed her cheek and quietly sat by her on the bed, holding her hand. The last thing she said to me before dozing off was, "Martin did it the right way." Twenty years before, her husband, Martin, had been diagnosed with cancer. He took a gun and shot himself.

I sat there for awhile, hoping Jean wouldn't have too much pain.

Dying is so awful. Why couldn't doctors have just given her a pill when the cancer returned? And then the thought: How is it going to be for me? Can I do this differently?

On Monday afternoon, the call came: Jean had died that morning.

End-of-Life Issues

A year later, my 91-year-old husband, Bob, fell desperately ill and had to be hospitalized. At 2 a.m., I drove home for a much-needed nap.

I had just fallen asleep when my cellphone rang. It was the intensive care doctor who had seen my husband for the first time, calling to ask what procedures I would allow him to perform.

Did he have my permission to put Bob on a ventilator or use a defibrillator?

I immediately arranged for a cab to get back to the hospital.

For almost two years, my husband and I had been living in a retirement community, Vi at Highlands Ranch. We had been watching older people struggle to remain alive. One woman had a stroke and was unable to talk or walk and was sustained by a feeding tube.

We had seen some of our new friends have successful operations, only to be followed by staph infections, blood clots and pulmonary complications.

Bob and I frequently talked about end-of-life issues. The question we struggled with was how much suffering we should endure to remain alive. We filled out an Advanced Care Directive, which committed our beliefs to writing. And I had given paramedics that information when the ambulance took him to the hospital.

Fortunately, we had had those discussions; they gave me the strength to assert our beliefs when the ICU [intensive care unit] physician called.

Death by Treatment of Pain

Once back at the hospital, I remained by my husband's side. He was suffering so much. I finally said to the ICU nurse, "Can't you give him something to relieve his suffering?" She said he could have morphine, but then they would no longer be able to treat him aggressively.

At that point, it would have been nice if a medical professional had offered to discuss Bob's care options with me. It was clear the nurse was not going to advise me.

Yet I felt certain that my husband would not get well again. "Give him morphine."

When the morphine started to work, relief registered on Bob's face, as well as mine and our daughter's.

In retrospect I realize the decision was not nearly as rational as it sounds here. I'm not sure I really knew that choosing morphine was signing his death certificate. I just knew then that it was the right thing for Bob.

What is wrong with giving up or giving in when our bodies can no longer hold up?

Bob died peacefully 12 hours after they began the morphine. Later, we discovered it was highly unlikely that he could have survived the bacterial infection. If he had, his quality of life would have been seriously compromised.

My mourning the loss of my husband is tempered by knowing I made the right decision for him.

I don't get it: Why are so many older people afraid to die? We know we can't live forever. What is wrong with giving up or giving in when our bodies can no longer hold up?

I've learned a lot through Jean's death and then Bob's death. I hope my experience will help older people, their adult kids and doctors become more confident in making end-of-life choices.

Rejecting Physician-Assisted Suicide in All Situations Relies on Faulty Moral Reasoning

Constantine A. Manthous is a clinical professor of medicine at Yale University School of Medicine and director of medical intensive care at Bridgeport Hospital.

Physician-assisted suicide and euthanasia are topics that engender a strong negative response on the part of many physicians and patients. This article explores contributions of religion, Western medical mores, law, and emerging concepts of moral neurocognition that may explain our inherent aversion to these ideas. The central thesis is that our collective repudiation of physician-assisted suicide (PAS) and euthanasia are moral intuitions, without rational foundation, predicated on inherited, self-preserving neurocircuitry. We, who are physically and mentally well, cannot empathize with patients who experience irreversible suffering unto death; euthanasia is anathema to our self-preservation instinct. Religious, cultural, and moral-legal indoctrination reflect and actualize our natural intuitions against euthanasia. Nonetheless, rational consideration may yield greater insight and perhaps different conclusions. If great care is taken to ensure that a request for physician-assisted death is persistent despite exhaustion of all available therapeutic modalities, then an argument can be made that our rejection constrains unnecessarily the liberty of a small number of patients.

A follow-up to the End of Life Practices in European Intensive Care Units Study (ETHICUS) suggests that clinicians intended to therapeutically expedite death in up to 18% of

Constantine A. Manthous, "Why Not Physician-Assisted Death?," *Critical Care Medicine*, vol. 37, no. 4, April 2009, pp. 1206–1209.

patients whose life-sustaining therapies were withdrawn. ETHICUS investigators reported that active shortening of the dying process (SDP)—a term borrowed from previous studies—was often difficult to distinguish from therapies intended to relieve pain and suffering because clinicians' intentions "are often difficult to ascertain." Experts have argued that while medications used to achieve comfort may accelerate death, the clinician's intent is the "bright line" that separates permissible palliative care from SDP that is prohibited in most jurisdictions. Despite prohibitions, some ETHICUS respondents covertly ignored that bright line, admitting that their intent was to simultaneously attenuate suffering *and* hasten deaths of their critically ill patients.

An argument can be made that our rejection [of assisted suicide] constrains unnecessarily the liberty of a small number of patients.

Although SDP described in ETHICUS was confined to critically ill dying patients, implicit is the broader question of why clinicians should or should not intend to hasten death. In abstract, SDP includes PAS and euthanasia. In PAS, which is legal in Switzerland and the State of Oregon, medications are prescribed but doctors do not administer them. Euthanasia, which is legal in the Netherlands and Belgium, allows clinicians to administer medications that hasten death. All forms of hastened death share one attribute: they are taboo in most societies. Why did so many European physicians admit to defying the taboo to ease the passing of their critically ill patients? Were they acting in the best interests of their patients? This article explores how religion, Western medical mores, Western legal concepts (specifically, embodied in the U.S. Constitution) and, possibly, moral neurocognition contribute to our discomfort with hastening death.

As a general rule, holy books of the major religions are relatively vague about hastening the death of another, whereas religious institutions' interpretations and prescriptions (with or without citation) are definitive. Western societies, including the United States, are founded on Judeo-Christian principles. Although the fifth of the Ten Commandments is "Thou shall not kill," there is no explicit mention of assisted suicide. There are also passages in which a supplicant begs God for death, but there is no mention of a response condoning or prohibiting suicide or assisted suicide.

Church Teachings

Despite lack of definitive guidance from the Bible, the Catholic Church has offered very explicit guidelines. The Church prohibits withholding of food and hydration for patients with advance dementia, vegetative states, etc., insofar as it is intended to cause the patient's death.

> "The will and action taken to cause a person's death is an act of murder. Those who are suffering and are nearing death must be allowed to die (or recover, which is sometimes a possibility) naturally. Administration of painkillers is permissible, provided the drugs are not willed as an end or means to precipitate death."

In his encyclical Evangelium Vitae, Pope John Paul [II] denounces individuals and states that take action which shortens life. For devout Catholics, SDP, in all forms, is considered a sin.

There are a number of denominations in the Protestant faith that do not speak with one voice. Protestant churches in the Netherlands united to oppose legalization of euthanasia there. The Archbishop of Canterbury has spoken against SDP/PAS and, in general, Protestants do not condone SDP. The Eastern Orthodox Church similarly rejects SDP.

There is no direct mention of euthanasia or assisted suicide in the Koran. The prohibition for killing (except in war) is mentioned in numerous passages including:

> You shall not kill any person—for GOD has made life sacred—except in the course of justice.

Proponents might suggest that of SDP/PAS/euthanasia are not killing and that it is just to aid a suffering person, even in hastening death. The Koran also explicitly prohibits suicide:

> Do not kill yourselves. God is merciful to you, but he that does that through wickedness and injustice shall be burned in fire.

Although there is no mention whether PAS or euthanasia would be permissible for suffering and terminal disease, one review suggests they are prohibited.

Other Eastern religions are not definitively prescriptive. Hindus are likely to oppose PAS and euthanasia, whereas the position of Buddhists is less clear.

Ultimately, the debate distills to the proper goals of medicine: to maintain bodily function or to serve overall well being, including autonomy, of the individual.

Tenets of Western medicine are concordant with ethical-legal constructs that prohibit physicians' prescriptions to expedite death. In the Hippocratic Oath, physicians are obliged to "neither give a deadly drug to anybody who asked for it, nor will I make a suggestion to this effect." Nonetheless, suicide was not uniformly prohibited in some ancient societies:

> "Suicide was not censured in antiquity. Self-murder as a relief from illness was regarded as justifiable, so much so that in some states it was an institution duly legalized by the authorities. Nor did ancient religion proscribe suicide. It did not know of any eternal punishment for those who ended

their own lives. Law and religion then left the physician free to do whatever his conscience allowed."

"Pythagoreanism is the only dogma that can possibly account for the attitude advocated in the Hippocratic Oath. Among all the Greek philosophical schools, the Pythagoreans alone outlawed suicide and abortion and did so without qualification."

Dr. Sherwin Nuland has argued that taking the Hippocratic Oath, although a traditional rite of passage, is not absolute and does not relieve doctors of their ethical obligations to consider the appropriateness of various medical techniques. Ultimately, the debate distills to the proper goals of medicine: to maintain bodily function or to serve overall well being, including autonomy, of the individual.

Harold Sox recently described the evolution of professionalism in Western medicine, culminating in the American College of Physicians' Charter of Medical Professionalism, a modern-day Hippocratic Oath, that states:

"Physicians must have respect for patient autonomy. Physicians must be honest with their patients and empower them to make informed decisions about their treatment. Patients' decisions about their care must be paramount, as long as those decisions are in keeping with ethical practice and do not lead to demands for inappropriate care."

But are PAS and euthanasia ethical and appropriate? Both the American College of Physicians and American Medical Association have taken the position that both are inappropriate. They argue that requests for PAS and euthanasia result from insufficient palliative care. Furthermore, PAS would "probably broaden to include nonconsenting and nonterminally ill persons." However, this "slippery slope" argument has not, to date, been validated in Oregon, where fewer than 50 cases/year of PAS have occurred since inception of its statute in 1996. Even when the door is opened, patients have not "run for it" (see potential teleological explanation below). And for some patients, just knowing the door is open—that they have some control—is palliative. . . .

Moral Neurocognition

Emerging concepts in cognition and moral psychology may help explain opposition to SDP across societies, cultures, and religions. Neuro and behavioral scientists have observed that humans have a "first take" on moral issues—i.e., they rapidly process a conundrum and come to an initial conclusion. The trolley metaphor is commonly used to illustrate this idea. If a train is barreling down the tracks and approaches a fork—on one side there is one person walking on the tracks, whereas on the other side there are five—most (85%) of subjects find it morally acceptable to flip a switch to send the train down the track-of-one, sacrificing the one for the five. However, few (12%) choose to push one in the way of the train if it could prevent dispatch of the five, despite the fact that the end result is identical. Functional imaging studies have begun to identify areas of the brain dedicated to moral cognition. This rapid, super-rational sensibility is termed *"moral intuition,"* in distinction to "moral reasoning" in which we take more time to apply rational principles to reach a conclusion.

> *Self-preservation is the dominant conserved theme in the hierarchy of our neurocognitive evolutionary legacy.*

Just as Noam Chomsky has argued that there are structural and functional neural templates for language in all humans, moral psychologists argue that a similar template—a shared "moral grammar"—has evolved for humans. A majority rapidly answers that pushing one to save five is unacceptable but cannot explain why it differs from flipping a switch with the same result—a manifestation of the moral grammar. Although physically pushing the victim may engender a more proximate relationship with the "thou shalt not kill" taboo, moral psychologists argue that this processing is entirely unconscious and neurally determined. Accumulating data from human and primate experiments support this hypothesis. Proponents, like Marc Hauser and Frans de Waal, have taken these arguments beyond the scientific community, directly to the public.

Self-preservation is the dominant conserved theme in the hierarchy of our neurocognitive evolutionary legacy. Evolutionary theorists suggest that most traits persist because they confer adaptive advantages, i.e., are self- or species-preserving. Pleasure is a physiologic drive that is highly represented in our neural architecture and repertoire of behaviors and liberty is the vehicle for pleasure. Many pleasurable activities—eating, copulating, exercise—serve self-preservation or preservation of the species. A third force, which also complements self-preservation, is cooperative behavior in groups. The Golden Rule is a principle that is conserved over nearly all cultures and religions—an adaptive advantage, passed on to us (collectively). Moral psychology suggests that these, and other, themes are hard-wired into our moral grammar.

Nature and Nurture

States and religions are human constructs, which organize individuals providing adaptive advantage by simultaneously promoting the interests of individuals comprising the collective and of the collective itself. Accordingly, it follows that religions and states—if they to varying degrees institutionalize our neurocognitive heritage—reflect our hard-wiring. It is, thus, reasonable to posit that formal strictures of tribal values, derived from inherited neurocircuitry, are tabulated in religious edicts and legal systems. Religion and states are instruments for enunciating (and enforcing) the moral imperatives and grammar produced through eons of brain evolution.

Thus, there is room in this formulation for both nature and nurture to determine our moral selves. Our inherited neurologic circuitry is a template that is "finished" by institutional indoctrination which fires that circuitry repetitively throughout our development (e.g., thou shalt not kill, thou shalt not kill, *ad infinitum*). It both feels right and, when fully indoctrinated, is programmed into the fully moral individual. There is a very large literature suggesting that during "critical periods" of brain development, environmental triggers (language for example) act on the neural template to potentiate development of particular skills or behaviors. Although evidence remains circumstantial (e.g., in primate studies), developing morality may follow a similar paradigm.

We might consider examining more carefully, beyond our intuition and indoctrination, whether our collective repudiation of [shortening of the dying process] is justified.

Accordingly, my thesis here is that our repudiation of PAS and euthanasia is a moral intuition, without rational foundations. On any given day, the majority of "us," i.e., doctors, patients, relatively well persons go about our normal activities and the self-preservation theme is dominant. There are some who want to die, but whose condition *is* reversible with medical, psychological, or other interventions. We reason that the "slippery slope" of PAS might sweep them inappropriately to death. Yet, unarguably there are also some patients, who are suffering and who *have* exhausted all modalities. The quality of their lives as they die (at varying velocities) is not acceptable to them. The American Medical Association and American College of Physicians assert that these individuals *can* be treated successfully, if greater attention is brought to bear. But some situations cannot be treated or reversed. Is this tyranny of the majority appropriate?

Toward a Solution

So for the moment, let the reader suspend gut revulsion to SDP, PAS, and euthanasia. At this point in our "moral history," the words themselves are polarizing. In this way, Noam Chomsky's ideas of language and moral psychologists' ideas of moral intuition converge. If test subjects in the trolley experiment are asked whether they would flip a switch to *slaughter* one to save the five, the frequency of responses will certainly differ. Similarly, the words *euthanasia* and *physician-assisted suicide* cause "gut reactions" that are independent of the rational credibility of the arguments. Nature, i.e., our hard-wired discomfort with promoting death is amplified by nurture, i.e., religious, medical and legal prohibitions. Words trigger neurologic phenomenon that correlate to moral tenets. In this way, deliberations might benefit from alternative terminology, say, "physician-assisted death for irreversible suffering."

Because it engenders such a visceral reaction, SDP is ideal for pondering the more general question: from whence our morals? This prism can be used to assess a variety of medical ethical conundrums. Moral psychology (nature) *and* institutionalized indoctrination (nurture) may explain our inherent discomfort with SDP in all its forms. If our role as physicians is to treat patients as a bundle of organs, then SDP should remain anathema to our values. However, if our role is to treat the patient as an abstract entity that includes body and soul, and if we truly believe that autonomy should be respected, then we might consider examining more carefully, beyond our intuition and indoctrination, whether our collective repudiation of SDP is justified. The data presented by ETHICUS investigators suggest that in Europe these deliberations have begun at the individual level. As the U.S. population ages, and a generation accustomed to medical autonomy face death, the public is beginning to ask these questions. As in Oregon, this process is best served by open consensus-driven illumination. After consideration, some states' citizens may conclude that the risks of PAS exceed the benefit to so few who would use it. Others, like the citizens of Oregon, may disagree. However, insofar as SDP, to varying degrees, is already occurring, irrespective of best intentions, it must not be provided at the caprice of individuals. The potential for abuse and arbitrary application is too great.

Active Euthanasia Is Never Morally Justified

Doug McManaman

Doug McManaman is a deacon and a religion and philosophy teacher at Father Michael McGivney Catholic Academy in Ontario, Canada.

Language that has been used in support of a Bill to legalize euthanasia has almost always been worded so as to appear most humane. Words such as "compassion," "autonomy," "dignity," and expressions like "medical assistance in dying" or "medically recommended course of treatment" often pad the arguments and, unfortunately, deceive the unwary. Consider the expression: "medical assistance in dying", or "medically recommended course of treatment". The word "medical" comes from the Latin *medicor*, which means "to heal." To make someone die, by lethal injection for example, is not medical at all, despite it being administered by a medical doctor, but is radically anti-medical. There are many linguistic traps like these, which is why we should become familiar with some of the basic principles of Catholic Life Ethics to help us see through some of the arguments of those who belong to the culture of death.

First, we need to keep in mind that over the past 40 years, there has been a subtle change in the way we as a culture regard human life. Within this period, we can discern two competing attitudes towards human life; the one is the Sanctity of Life mentality, which at one time dominated the medical profession, the other is the Quality of Life mentality, which seems to be more widespread today.

The *Sanctity of Life* mentality regards individual human life as holy, sacred, and of immeasurable value, regardless of the physical and/or mental quality of the person. You can place a price on things, but not on human persons who are created by God and who are called by God, each one, to union with Him in the unimaginable joy of eternal life in heaven.

The *Quality of Life* mentality does not see individual human life as holy, sacred, of immeasurable value, but actually places a value on individual human life on the basis of its physical and/or mental quality, as we would place a price on a product. We value computers and automobiles on the basis of their quality, whether they function well, whether they are useful and efficient. The Quality of Life mentality places a higher value on a human life that is of greater physical and mental quality, and a lesser value on individual human life that is of lesser physical and mental quality. And so a handicapped child would be of less value than a healthy child. In this framework, human persons are valued for their productivity, their ability to be of some use to society as a whole, not for their own sake.

Over the past 40 years, there has been a subtle change in the way we as a culture regard human life.

The Christian world has always rejected this. Every individual person has been created by God, each one of us, for Himself, not for our parents, not for the State, but for eternal union with Himself, because He loves us individually, and He loves us as if there is only one of us. God entrusts children to parents, but first and foremost, they belong to God.

Of course God calls each person to serve the common good of the civil community to the extent of his ability, but each person has been given life for his own sake. And Christ is mysteriously united to every individual person, because that same God who created us joined a human nature and with it redeemed us all. Christ sacrifices himself so that we might have life. But those who belong to the culture of death have the reverse attitude: they believe it is acceptable to sacrifice individual human life in order to make their own temporary lives here more convenient.

The Value of Life

This attitude of the culture of death spread rapidly after the legalization of abortion, and many social critics predicted that infanticide would soon follow—which is the deliberate starvation and neglect of handicapped children whose lives are deemed not worth living. We saw this come to pass in the famous Baby Doe case back in April of 1982 in Bloomington, Indiana. Infanticide has been happening ever since, here in Canada as well as elsewhere in Europe.

Critics also pointed out that the next target, after infants, will be the terminally ill and the elderly. To help this along, we have seen a gradual redefining of the terms, in particular "murder." The western world has always understood murder to be the intentional killing of another human being. That the murdered victim wanted to die was and is entirely irrelevant. If I shoot a student who asked me to end his life, with his own gun, the fact that he willed to die does not change the fact that I carried out an act with the intent to bring an end to his life. That is murderous. But what is happening today is that murder is being defined as killing someone against his/her will.

We, of course, do not accept this. My will does not alter the value of my life. Human life itself is sacred, intrinsically good, whether the person is sick, dying, terminally ill, whether he wants to live or not, whether he is mentally ill, depressed, or mentally handicapped, or quadriplegic.

There are two types of euthanasia, *active and passive.* Active euthanasia is death by commission. A person is given a lethal injection, for example, or the doctor mixes a lethal cocktail for the patient to drink. Passive euthanasia is death by omission. A person dies because a certain medical treatment is omitted or withdrawn.

Ordinary and Extraordinary Treatment

Active euthanasia is very simple from a moral point of view. It is never justified, because it always amounts to murder. It is the intentional destruction of human life, which is intrinsically good and of immeasurable value, regardless of the condition of the patient. Passive euthanasia, however, can sometimes be justified, depending on the circumstances. Here is where we have to tread carefully. At this point we need to distinguish between two types of treatment: extraordinary and ordinary treatment.

Extraordinary treatment is any medical treatment that is a *serious* burden on the patient either physically, psychologically, emotionally, or even financially. Ordinary treatment is any medical treatment that is not a serious burden on the patient physically, or psychologically, or emotionally, or financially.

Human life itself is sacred, intrinsically good, whether the person is sick, dying, terminally ill, whether he wants to live or not,whether he is mentally ill, depressed, or mentally handicapped.

Traditional medical ethics and Catholic teaching have always taught that one is obligated to use ordinary treatment to preserve human life. But one is not obligated to use extraordinary treatment to preserve human life. If a treatment is a serious burden on the patient in one of the aforementioned ways and he refuses it because it is seriously burdensome, he is not thereby intending his own death. He is accepting his death as a side effect of refusing a seriously burdensome treatment. Suppose a doctor were to tell a person that he has six months to live, but that with a treatment that carries seriously painful or psychologically repugnant side effects, his life can be extended for an extra two years or so. A person does not necessarily have an obligation to consent to it. Again, what the person intends is not necessarily the ending of his own life, but the ending or impeding of a medical treatment that is seriously burdensome in some way. Death is a side effect of removing such treatment, and death is accepted, not intended.

But some people omit ordinary treatment *so that* the patient will die. We saw this in Missouri, with the Nancy Cruzan case. The parents pushed to have the feeding tube removed, not because it was a serious burden, but because they couldn't stand to see their daughter in a persistent vegetative state. The tube was removed so that she would die. Her death was intended, and this is murder.

It is never justified to intentionally bring an end to human life in order to relieve one of a burdensome existence.

We need also to be careful of what some call extraordinary treatment. High tech medical equipment is not necessarily extraordinary treatment. The definition of extraordinary is such that what is ordinary here in Canada might very well be extraordinary in the United States. As circumstances change, so too might the status of a medical treatment. What is ordinary treatment for a young 40-year-old, such as a form of chemotherapy, might constitute extraordinary treatment for a 77-year-old man whose body may not be able to recover as well as that of a younger man.

Performing CPR [cardiopulmonary resuscitation] on a young teenager whose heart has stopped is usually ordinary treatment. A young man can recover from the injuries to his rib cage resulting from CPR, but an 86-year-old grandmother in a Palliative Care Unit who has already been resuscitated once before might find the physical side effects of CPR far too burdensome. Her decision in favour of a *Do Not Resuscitate Order* is not necessarily suicidal. Rather, she is accepting her own death. She intends to be delivered from a treatment that she finds seriously burdensome physically. That, of course, is very different from removing all treatment because one does not wish to live with a disease, or one does not want a child who is disabled.

A Serious Burden

Those who promote euthanasia will often use the words "serious burden." If we look closely at what exactly is the serious burden, however, we see that it is not the medical treatment at all, but the condition of the patient. It is never justified to intentionally bring an end to human life in order to relieve one of a burdensome existence. To do so is to do evil to achieve good. Our obligation is to love our patients, not for our sake, but for theirs, to care for them even when they cannot thank us or when they are not apparently aware of us. Our duty is to make them as comfortable as possible, to reduce pain as much as possible, even if such pain management has, as an undesirable side effect, the shortening of a person's life. In this case, we accept that side effect. But we must not eliminate the pain by intentionally eliminating the patient.

Individual human life is intrinsically good, holy, created by God and of immeasurable value, and it is to be revered absolutely. Much of the darkness that covers this world is rooted in our refusal to love individual human life absolutely and for its own sake. But life will be brighter for all of us when we begin to take concrete steps to reverse this trend.

CHAPTER 3

Does Assisted Suicide Lead to Abuses?

Chapter Preface

In the debate over assisted suicide, a recurring issue for both sides is whether social acceptance of the practice leads to abuses. Consideration of potential harms is relevant in deciding whether assisted suicide should be legalized or decriminalized. On the one hand, some opponents are against assisted suicide because they believe that taking one's life is immoral or against religion. On the other hand, assisted suicide can be opposed on more practical grounds—because of the perceived negative consequences of the act.

If the acceptance of assisted suicide means that people are harmed as a result—either directly or indirectly—there may be reason to oppose the acceptance or legalization of assisted suicide. One of the frequent objections to legalizing assisted suicide is that such social acceptance will lead to a "slippery slope," in which the practice will be expanded to include circumstances not originally intended. Opponents of assisted suicide often voice several concerns that the act, once legalized, cannot be contained. First, there is the concern that allowing the terminally ill to end their lives by assisted suicide will slowly be expanded to include anyone who wants to die—ill or not. Second, there is the worry that allowing people to "choose" assisted suicide will devolve into people being pressured into "choosing" suicide, thus widening the number of people who die. Third, there is a more general worry that social acceptance of assisted suicide will lead to social acceptance of other life-ending acts, such as suicide, euthanasia, and even murder. Here the concern is that acceptance of a particular kind of hastening of death will expand to include other hastenings, if not outright killings.

Any time the slippery slope charge is made, there is a risk of the so-called slippery slope fallacy, where the charge of ensuing consequences has no rational basis. An extreme example of this would be the claim that if you sanction assisted suicide, soon we will all be dead. The leap from the allowance of assisted suicide to the death of all people is clearly not supported by any evidence. In the case of the slippery slope arguments against assisted suicide, then, the reasons for the alleged consequences must be examined to determine whether they are justified and based on a rational assessment of likely outcomes.

Just as opponents of assisted suicide sometimes claim that the practice, once legalized, cannot be contained and will lead to negative, unintended consequences, proponents of assisted suicide maintain that the prohibition against the practice is what leads to negative consequences. Central to many of these arguments is the notion of autonomy, or self-governance. When society limits the freedom of individuals to take their own lives, it limits their autonomy. If there are no abuses to worry about, however, then the limitation on individual autonomy can become an unjustified abuse itself.

Looking at the arguments for and against the idea that assisted suicide leads to abuses, or harms, is an important component of the debate about assisted suicide. Consequences matter, and identifying the accurate outcomes of the social acceptance of assisted suicide can make all the difference.

Assisted Suicide Puts People with Disabilities at the Greatest Risk

Mark P. Mostert

Mark P. Mostert is director of the Institute for the Study of Disability and Bioethics at Regent University School of Education in Virginia.

We are at a critical juncture in the fight against death-making. Acceptance of assisted suicide is likely to increase now that it has been legalized in Oregon and Washington state; similar initiatives have been proposed across the rest of the U.S. It is likely that increased social acceptance of assisted suicide (and, eventually, euthanasia) will continue to reinforce several dangerous pro-death ideas, including the basic notion that we can do away with people just as we rid ourselves of old, worn-out, or otherwise imperfect possessions. Such tectonic [fundamental] shifts in attitude will inevitably mean that our most vulnerable populations, including and especially people with disabilities, will be seen as disposable. . . .

Most people view death as the last stage of the existential cycle of life, a universal rhythm ensuring a living communal humanity into the future. It is this fundamental notion that shapes, in part, the powerful urge to procreate, to leave a living legacy after we're gone, and to grapple with what death means and how we should approach it. It is not possible, therefore, to consider the human condition without the understanding that death is an inevitable part of what we are. However, in the context of assisted suicide and euthanasia, I make a fundamental distinction between natural death and my notion of "death-making."

Mark P. Mostert, "Opposing 'The Propaganda of the Deed': Eugenic Death-Making and the Disabled," *Human Life Review*, vol. 35, no. 4, Fall 2009, pp. 73–82.

Death-making is very different from death's simply *happening*, although the result is the same. Death-making implies an action; it preempts the natural course of events. Death-making is the chief characteristic of assisted suicide and the hallmark of euthanasia. Its purpose is making one who is living, *dead*. On this point, there is surely little disagreement. Further, death-making is a stealthily destructive act because it masquerades as compassion and care, a deceptive logic declaring that death-making is for the best, an act of true and unselfish benevolence, and a way of acknowledging that because life isn't the same as it used to be, it needs to be terminated.

A Domino Effect

Across the world, countries, like so many dominoes, have fallen, one after the other, to the lowest common denominator—that making people dead is acceptable and, in some quite deranged corners of the planet, that it should be required, and even celebrated. Thus, we are on the cusp of an unprecedented development that was previously unthinkable, even in our own lifetimes: The pro-death lobby has twisted societal thinking from seeing assisted suicide and euthanasia as unethical or immoral in almost every instance to beginning to view death-making as a legitimate ritual.

Rituals consist of a social set of behaviors and events determining social conduct. I believe we are at a place where death-making is becoming a ritual like marriage or burial. This is how it works: A "capable" person voluntarily expresses his or her wish to die because of some terminal or hopeless illness. A physician (and perhaps a second doctor) verifies the terminal or hopeless illness. The person requesting assisted suicide or euthanasia makes a witnessed, written, signed, and dated request for death so that medication can be prescribed for the purpose of ending life in a "humane and dignified" manner. The fatal medication is then obtained, and the patient chooses a time and place to die. The patient then takes the fatal dose, and dies.

There you have it: the ritual of assisted suicide. The same will be true when euthanasia is legalized and, eventually, socially accepted. And it is in this context of ritualized death-making that people with disabilities are likely to be among the first to succumb.

Death-making is the chief characteristic of assisted suicide and the hallmark of euthanasia.

There is no question that the developed world does more for people with disabilities than is done anywhere else. We have more laws, more accommodations, more advocacies, and more support for them than at any time in history. In the U.S., as in many other developed countries, people with disabilities are the largest minority group. Under various disability classifications, approximately 54 million Americans have at least one disability, and this number is expected to double in the next two decades.

Even this number includes only a portion of the disabled population. For example, classified differently, there are 133 million people in the U.S. living with a chronic health condition, and their numbers are projected to increase to 150 million by 2030. Seventy-five percent of people with chronic health conditions are younger than 65. Many will have chronic health conditions severe enough that, by any standard, they are medically disabled.

People with significant disabilities conveniently fit the aims of the pro-death agenda: They consume significant medical and other resources; they often have impaired quality of life and diminished autonomy; in many instances, they suffer greatly. I cannot think of a more vulnerable group, who will be increasingly targeted for death.

Here's my blunt paraphrase of how the pro-death lobby will rationalize death-making for people with medical and other disabilities: "Your medical and support care costs too much. By virtue of your disability, you have a poor quality of life. You suffer many indignities and struggles that leave you feeling worthless or a burden on others. You are largely invisible to the rest of society. You suffer a great deal physically, psychologically, in how your life is playing out. We can help you end your misery at a time of your choosing and in a comfortable and dignified way."

Ritualized death-making and people with significant disabilities are the essential ingredients for an old but still vibrant idea: eugenic euthanasia.

The Rise of Eugenics

Eugenics started out as a fairly benevolent *what if?* In the 19th century, [Gregor] Mendel's genetic breakthroughs established that it was possible to predict characteristics of living things by selective breeding. It didn't take long to make the logical jump from Mendel's sweet peas to the genetic makeup of man, and the idea that it was possible to genetically breed better people, and, conversely, to "breed out" less desirable human qualities.

One faction of eugenicists stuck closely to the natural-selection idea, that nature itself would weed out defectives over time. Others took a more active position, suggesting that societies engage in "positive" eugenics—that is, that people with desirable traits be encouraged to procreate. It wasn't much of a stretch from positive eugenics to its opposite: that those with less desirable characteristics should be actively dissuaded from procreating, whether by propaganda, by law, or, even more actively, by widespread sterilization.

At that same time, killing via euthanasia was widely debated, for a simple reason: Sterilization itself only partially addressed the issue of ridding society of potential defectives because it did not address what to do with those defectives already inconveniently alive. Their very existence was an affront to the highbrow ideals of perfection and a "better society for all."

Ritualized death-making and people with significant disabilities are the essential ingredients for an old but still vibrant idea: eugenic euthanasia.

In *The Black Stork*, Martin Pernick notes that the convergence of eugenics and euthanasia can be traced back as far as 1868, and that by 1890 national debates on the killing of defectives were taking place both in the U.S. and in Europe. Newborns with disabilities were the first targeted, but soon the killing idea moved beyond infants. In Hungary, child-welfare pioneer Sigmund Engel demanded that "cripples, high-grade cretins, idiots, and children with gross deformities . . . should be quickly and painlessly destroyed [when] medical science indicates, beyond the possibility of a doubt that it is impossible for them ever to become useful members of society [or when] it is obvious that their existence is directly harmful to the species."

Some people who should have known better went along with these suggestions. For example Alfred Nobel, the Swedish inventor, himself a man with a disability, acknowledged the appropriateness of infanticide, and that he himself should have been terminated. Nobel described himself as a "pitiful creature [who] ought to have been suffocated by a humane physician when he made his howling entrance into this life."

Similar sentiments turned up in the United States. In 1899, Simeon Baldwin, a Yale law professor and incoming president of the American Social Sciences Association, used his presidential address to oppose surgery on newborns with disabilities if the "operation can only save the life by making it a daily and hopeless misery." State legislators pressed home this idea. In 1903, Michigan state representative Link Rogers proposed a law to electrocute mentally defective infants. In 1906, both Ohio and Iowa saw similar legislative debates over proposed euthanasia laws, include killing "lunatics and idiots."

Thus, for well over a century, eugenics and euthanasia have walked hand in hand. Currently, we see the results of eugenic euthanasia in the termination of Down syndrome and other pregnancies deemed genetically imperfect, the euthanasia of the elderly and medically disabled in Europe, and the increasing pressure to equate acceptable quality of life with human perfection.

The Propaganda of the Deed

Proponents of death-making have not gotten this far by accident. They are effectively persuading the unsuspecting public with an impressive combination of shock tactics, agitprop [political propaganda disseminated through the arts], and intolerance for dissent. In sum, they have shown great skill in using a powerful form of activist influence known as *the propaganda of the deed*: the execution of certain actions for their psychological effect on the group of people one is trying to persuade. Most often, it is used to force a previously hidden social taboo into the public eye, thereby shifting the parameters of the debate by in-your-face tactics meant to shock, disgust, and, most important, to desensitize the public to the point where the taboo action is tolerated and eventually accepted. The intent is to (a) get people's attention, (b) heighten their awareness of an issue, (c) control the ensuing debate, and (d) by relentless public pressure, to force acceptance of the previously unacceptable.

Perhaps the prime examples of the propaganda of the deed in this debate were Jack Kevorkian's televised killing of Thomas Youk on CBS's *60 Minutes* in 1998, and the judicial execution of Terri Schiavo in 2005. In both instances, the taboo of suicide, assisted or otherwise, and especially in relation to persons with significant disabilities, was forcefully thrust from the shadows into the public consciousness.

Two prominent pro-death figures that are highly skilled in executing the propaganda of the deed are Baroness Mary Warnock and Professor Peter Singer.

Baroness Mary Warnock

In late 2008, Baroness Warnock, a former headmistress, commission chair, and perfectly sane woman, raised more than a few eyebrows with her comments on people's duty to die, as reported in the London *Telegraph*: "I'm absolutely, fully in agreement with the argument that if pain is insufferable, then someone should be given help to die, but I feel there's a wider argument, that if somebody absolutely, desperately wants to die because they're a burden to their family, or the state, then I think they too should be allowed to die. . . . There's nothing wrong with feeling you ought to do so for the sake of others as well as yourself. . . . I think that's the way the future will go, putting it rather brutally, you'd be licensing people to put others down."

Two prominent pro-death figures that are highly skilled in executing the propaganda of the deed are Baroness Mary Warnock and Professor Peter Singer.

The breathtaking sweep of these statements is self-evident, their implications, on many levels, alarming. But Warnock has been saying these things for years. In December 1994, London's *Sunday Times* described her as "Britain's leading medical ethics expert . . . [who has] suggested that the frail and elderly should consider suicide to stop them becoming a financial burden on their families and society." The paper quoted Warnock as saying: "I know I'm not really allowed to say it, but one of the things that would motivate me [to die] is I couldn't bear hanging on and being such a burden on people. . . . In other contexts, sacrificing oneself for one's family would be considered good. I don't see what is so horrible about the motive of not wanting to be an increasing nuisance. . . . If I went into a nursing home it would be a terrible waste of money that my family could use far better."

This is the same Baroness Warnock who previously made the case for parents being forced to pay for their infants' medical care, including for life-support equipment, if those infants were judged to have little to no chance of leading healthy lives. It's also the same Baroness Warnock who gladly endorses euthanasia and openly admits that the family doctor euthanized her husband several years ago. I found the level of outrage over Lady Warnock's latest comments somewhat surprising. At least she's consistent: What she wants for everyone else she enthusiastically embraced for her husband. In this I find her more credible than Peter Singer.

Professor Peter Singer

Singer's chilly utilitarianism clumsily reveals his naked prejudice against people with disabilities. Essentially, Singer thinks people with disabilities have less value than people who do not have a disability, that their quality of life is not as high, and that their lives are not as fulfilling as those of their non-disabled counterparts. He finds it permissible for parents to judge whether, according to *their* criteria, their child with a disability should live or die. He does concede, though, that children with Down syndrome are lovable and can be happy. I suppose these children should be grateful.

Singer bases his arguments on the presupposition that "life is better without a disability than with one, and this is not itself a form of prejudice." True, but it's not exactly a ringing endorsement either. Here's the way he views death-making of infants with disabilities: "We should certainly put very strict conditions on permissible infanticide; but these restrictions might owe more to the effects of infanticide on others than to the intrinsic wrongness of killing an infant."

In *Unsanctifying Human Life*, Singer argues that under many circumstances, people are just like any other animals, and that basically we should therefore consider treating imperfect humans just as we would imperfect animals. In this, at least, he's with Warnock and her ideas of "putting people down." But Singer, unlike Warnock, does not practice what he preaches. Several years ago, rather than euthanize his mother, who met all of *his own* criteria for doing so, Singer chose to spend significant amounts of money for her care until her natural death. Here's how he twisted out of it: "Well . . . it's probably not the best use you could make of my money. That is true. But it does provide employment for a number of people who find something worthwhile in what they're doing."

Warnock and Singer are the progeny of the same predecessors, including the infamous Dr. Harry Haiselden.

In the early 1900s, euthanizing defective infants by withholding treatment was quite common; however, it was done quietly on hospital back wards.

Dr. Harry Haiselden

In 1915, at the German-American hospital in Chicago, Anna Bollinger delivered a seven-pound baby boy. Allan had multiple disabilities: no neck, one ear, and severe chest and shoulder deformities. His pupils were slow to react to light, he did not have a rectal opening, he had a blocked bowel, and he had premature hardening of his skull and leg bones.

Haiselden, the hospital's eminent chief surgeon and an ardent eugenicist, knew that surgery could easily correct the blocked bowel and missing rectal opening. However, for Haiselden, Allan's other disabilities marked the infant for death. Haiselden recommended no surgery, and that the infant be left to die. Bowing to doctor power, the Bollingers agreed. Allan, naked, was moved to a bare room where Catherine Walsh, a family friend, found him: "Walsh had patted the infant lightly. Allan's eyes were open, and he waved his tiny fists at her. She kissed his forehead. 'I knew,' she recalled, 'if its mother got her eyes on it she would love it and never permit it to be left to die.'"

Walsh summoned Haiselden, she later said, "to beg that the child be taken to his mother." Her pleas fell on deaf ears. Begging the doctor once more, Walsh appealed to Haiselden's humanity: "If the poor little darling has one chance in a thousand," she pleaded, "won't you operate and save it?" No, Haiselden laughed, because "I'm afraid it might get well." Five days later, little Allan was dead.

In the early 1900s, euthanizing defective infants by withholding treatment was quite common; however, it was done quietly on hospital back wards. Haiselden realized that the time had come to force the issue into the open as a way of persuading the general public that eugenic euthanasia was not only acceptable, but even a considerate, loving act, and a civic responsibility. Quite the showman, Haiselden resorted to the propaganda of the deed to challenge, and then overpower, the taboo against the killing of newborns with severe medical and genetic disabilities. He succeeded.

The Popularity of Haiselden

The stories of little Allan and several other children who met the same fate exploded in the Chicago and national press. Haiselden was transformed into a cause célèbre overnight. The debate was furious, and, as would happen in Nazi Germany in the 1930s, it spurred pleas from parents across the country for Haiselden to do the same to their children with disabilities. A father in Des Moines, Iowa, wrote Haiselden about his two-month-old whose mouth and jaw were severely misshapen.

Contacted by the press, the father warned, "Unless someone does kill the baby, I'll have to." A mother in Baltimore, aware of Haiselden's views, was informed that her son needed triple amputation to save his life; she refused, commenting to the press that the child "should die rather than go through life a hopeless cripple."

> We must consistently and unfailingly refuse to be dissuaded from our central rallying position—that assisted suicide and eugenic euthanasia must be stopped, that living is a better alternative than the lie of a "dignified, good death," and we must articulate why it is morally, logically, and ethically wrong to devalue the most vulnerable among us.

The furor Haiselden caused finally resulted in a medical board of inquiry, at which he was acquitted. Asked by reporters whether what he had done was eugenic, Haiselden answered swiftly and decisively: "Eugenics? Of course it's eugenics," he said. Over the next several years, Haiselden vigorously promoted what he was doing in the press. He gave interviews incessantly, and was adept at co-opting props for his show: He frequently displayed dying infants to reporters and encouraged them to interview the still-hospitalized mothers. His propaganda of the deed convinced many; he had the very public support of the blind and deaf Helen Keller.

Haiselden's vigorous promotion of eugenic euthanasia culminated in perhaps the mother of all eugenic-propaganda films, *The Black Stork*. Often advertised as a "eugenic love story," it was later retitled *Are You Fit to Marry?* The film could still be found in movie theaters as late as 1942.

Haiselden, now Warnock and Singer, among many others. How might we stem this propagandistic tide?

We face immense struggles in an increasingly pro-death culture—a culture that, for example, sees clandestinely putting people to death in parking lots, as Dignitas [a Swiss-based association that helps people end their lives] has done in Switzerland, as some sort of weird moral breakthrough. It's a culture that has spawned the horror of the Netherlands, where assisted suicide and euthanasia are available to just about anyone who asks for them (and for many who do not). We are also witnessing the growing specter of *Eutho-tourism*, where people travel abroad to die, to say nothing of the utilitarian beast of "futile care." Moreover, the pro-death message from the news media is well-nigh universal: The narratives are often tinged with admiration, if not outright adulation. . . .

Addressing the Propaganda of the Deed

We must consistently and unfailingly refuse to be dissuaded from our central rallying position—that assisted suicide and eugenic euthanasia must be stopped, that living is a better alternative than the lie of a "dignified, good death," and we must articulate why it is morally, logically, and ethically wrong to devalue the most vulnerable among us.

We must do these things because hundreds of thousands of the vulnerable, the infirm, and the disabled cry out for our unity. They seek comfort and sanity. They are weak. They are sick. They are dying. They are human beings. They are of infinite value.

They deserve nothing but our best effort, because, in the end, they are us.

Decriminalizing Assisted Suicide Will Result in the Failure to Prosecute Killers

Wesley J. Smith

Wesley J. Smith is a senior fellow in human rights and bioethics at the Discovery Institute, a legal consultant to the Patients Rights Council, and a special consultant for the Center for Bio-ethics and Culture. He is the author of Forced Exit: Euthanasia, Assisted Suicide and the New Duty to Die.

On July 4, 1995, Myrna Lebov, age 52, committed suicide in her Manhattan apartment. The case generated national headlines when her husband, George Delury, announced that he had assisted Lebov's suicide at her request because she was suffering the debilitations of progressive multiple sclerosis.

Delury became an instant celebrity. He was acclaimed as a dedicated husband willing to risk jail to help his beloved wife achieve her desired end. The assisted-suicide movement set up a defense fund and renewed calls for legalization. Delury made numerous television appearances and was invited to speak to a convention of the American Psychiatric Association. He signed a deal for a book, later published under the title *But What If She Wants to Die?* Delury soon copped a plea to attempted manslaughter and served a few months in jail.

Had Delury acted in England or Wales today—rather than in New York in 1995—he almost surely would not have been prosecuted. Even though assisted suicide remains a crime in the U.K., newly published British guidelines have effectively decriminalized some categories of assisted suicide by instructing local prosecutors [that] bringing charges in such deaths is to be deemed "not in the public interest."

The guidelines were developed in response to a ruling by the U.K.'s highest court. A woman named Debbie Purdy—who like Lebov has progressive multiple sclerosis—plans to kill herself in one of Switzerland's suicide clinics if her suffering becomes too much to bear. Wanting to be accompanied by her husband, but fearful he could be prosecuted, she sued, demanding to be told by law enforcement ahead of time whether he would face charges.

Purdy won the day. Noting that other recent cases of "suicide tourism" (as such trips taken to Switzerland to die are called) had not been prosecuted, Britain's Law Lords ordered the head prosecutor to define the facts and circumstances under which the law would—and would not—be enforced.

The resulting guidelines declared that assisted suicides of people with a "terminal illness," a "severe and incurable disability," or "a severe degenerative physical condition"—whether occurring overseas or at home—should not be prosecuted if the assister was a close friend or relative of the deceased, was motivated by compassion, and the victim "had a clear, settled, and informed wish to commit suicide," among other criteria—exactly the circumstances Delury said motivated him to facilitate Lebov's death.

The Danger of Coercion

What do these guidelines teach us about assisted suicide? First, "death with dignity" is not just about terminal illness: It is about fear of disability and debilitation. A husband assisting the suicide of his wife, who wanted to die because their son became a quadriplegic, would be prosecuted under the guidelines, but he wouldn't face charges for assisting the suicide of the son.

Second, the guidelines prove that assisted suicide is not a medical act. Nothing in them requires a physician's review or participation.

Third, the court ruling and guidelines illustrate how the rule of law is crumbling. What matters most today is not principle, but emotion-driven personal narrative.

Perhaps most alarmingly, decriminalizing assisted suicide in these cases sends the insidious societal message that the lives of the dying and disabled are not as worthy of protecting as those of others. In this sense, the guidelines are an abandonment of society's most vulnerable citizens, exposing at least some to the acute danger of being coerced into death by relatives or friends.

Delury's Diary Entries

For proof, we need only turn again to George Delury. Here, as the late [radio commentator] Paul Harvey used to say, is the rest of the story.

Delury made a crucial mistake that changed his favorable public perception. Perhaps because he was planning to write a book, he kept a computer diary of the events leading up to Lebov's death—and its content shattered any pretense that he was motivated by love or compassion. To the contrary, George Delury put Myrna Lebov out of his misery.

The diary showed that Lebov did not have an unwavering and long-stated desire to die, as Delury had claimed. Rather, as often happens with people struggling with debilitating illnesses, her mood waxed and waned. One day she would be suicidal—but the next day she was engaged in life. Delury, moreover, encouraged his wife to kill herself, or as he put it, "to decide to quit." He researched her antidepressant medication to see if it could kill her, and when she took less than the prescribed amount, which in itself could cause depression, he stashed the surplus until he had enough for a poisonous brew.

That wasn't all. He worked assiduously at destroying Lebov's will to live by making her feel worthless and a burden. On March 28, 1995, Delury wrote in his diary that he planned to tell his wife:

> I have work to do, people to see, places to travel. But no one asks about my needs. I have fallen prey to the tyranny of a victim. You are sucking my life out of my [sic] like a vampire and nobody cares. In fact, it would appear that I am about to be cast in the role of villain because I no longer believe in you.

Delury later admitted on the NBC program *Dateline* that he had shown his wife that very passage.

Decriminalizing assisted suicide in these cases sends the insidious societal message that the lives of the dying and disabled are not as worthy of protecting as those of others.

That Delury wanted Lebov to kill herself is beyond dispute. On May 1 he wrote:

> Sheer hell. Myrna is more or less euphoric. She spoke of writing a book today. [Lebov was a published author, having written *Not Just a Secretary* in 1984.] She's interested in everything, wants everything explained, and believes that every bit of bad news has some way out. . . . It's all too much.

On June 10, Delury's diary described an argument with Lebov that started when she left a message to her niece that "things are looking splendid":

> I blew up! Shouting into the phone that everything was just the same, it was simply Myrna feeling different. I told Myrna that she had hurt me very badly, not my feelings, but physically and emotionally. "Now what will Beverly [Lebov's sister] think? That I'm lying about how tough things are here."

I put it to Myrna bluntly—"If you won't take care of me, I won't take care of you."

On July 3, 1995, the day before Myrna's death, Delury wrote:

Myrna is now questioning the efficacy of solution, a sure sign that she will not take [the overdose] tonight and doesn't want to. So, confusion and hesitation strike again. If she changes her mind tonight and does decide to go ahead, I will be surprised.

Finally, on July 4, Delury got what he wanted: Lebov swallowed the overdose of antidepressant medicine that her husband prepared for her and died.

Protecting the dying and infirm from assisted suicide is no longer in the public interest.

Once the contents of his diary were publicly revealed, though, Delury's defense of "compassion" became inoperative, which is why he accepted the bargain.

That still wasn't the end of the story. In *But What If She Wants to Die?*—published after double jeopardy prevented another prosecution—Delury wrote that he hadn't just mixed Lebov's drugs, but also smothered her with a plastic bag because he was worried that the amount she ingested might not be sufficient to kill her. Thus, Myrna Lebov didn't really die by suicide: She was killed by her husband. (Delury died by his own hand in 2007, at the age of 74.)

The Danger of Failing to Protect the Dying

Thanks to the assisted suicide guidelines, potential Myrna Lebovs in Britain are now at the mercy of future George Delurys. And those Delurys know full well that, so long as they don't keep inculpating diaries, they will have little trouble convincing prosecutors that their motive was compassion, a claim readily believed in a society so fearful and disdainful of disability. Such are the consequences of the state prosecutor's decision that protecting the dying and infirm from assisted suicide is no longer in the public interest.

People Will Be Encouraged to Die Because of Health Care Costs

Daniel Allott

Daniel Allott is a senior writer at American Values, a Washington fellow at the National Review Institute, and an executive producer of the documentary film Flashes of Color: Disability in the Age of Perfection.

Last June [2008] in Eugene, Oregon, 64-year-old Barbara Wagner received a letter from the state-run Oregon Health Plan. Wagner, who was suffering from a recurrence of lung cancer at the time, was informed that her health policy would not cover the high cost (about $4,000 a month) of her life-extending cancer drug.

"Treatment of advanced cancer that is meant to prolong life, or change the course of this disease, is not a covered benefit of the Oregon Health Plan," stated the letter Wagner received.

But the letter informed Wagner that the plan would cover the cost—only $50—of a much different treatment: doctor-assisted suicide.

"I think it's messed up," Wagner, who died in October, told reporters. "To say to someone, we'll pay for you to die, but not pay for you to live, it's cruel," she said. "I get angry. Who do they think they are?"

Such is life in Oregon, which, until recently, was the only state where physician-assisted suicide was legal.

Euthanasia occasionally resurfaces as a front-page news story. A decade ago, Jack Kevorkian made headlines when he was sent to prison for second-degree murder after assisting in a patient's suicide (though only after having assisted over 130 other patients to end their lives).

Four years ago this week [on March 31, 2005], Terri Schiavo's death by starvation and dehydration caused such a stir that it provoked our current president [Barack Obama] to commit what he would later call his "biggest mistake" in the U.S. Senate by voting for legislation allowing Schiavo's family to take its case from state courts to federal courts in an effort to stop her murder.

For the most part, though, euthanasia has remained a second-tier political issue, even in pro-life circles, where it has generally been subordinate to abortion, sex education, and stem cells.

The Growing Acceptance of Assisted Suicide

But that's about to change. Last November [2008], voters made Washington the second state to legalize physician-assisted suicide. In December, a Montana judge ruled euthanasia legal in that state. Meanwhile in Oregon, whose voters legalized euthanasia in 1994, a record 60 physician-assisted suicides were reported in 2008. This year, assisted suicide legalization bills have been introduced in Hawaii and New Hampshire.

Add to these developments the perfect storm of record budget shortfalls, a looming entitlements crisis fueled by scores of millions of baby boomers on the cusp of retirement and end of life, and a president and Congress that embrace a utilitarian view of human life, and it's easy to see why euthanasia is reemerging as a top issue. This time it might be here for good.

Advocates of assisted suicide like to talk about compassion and choice. But utilitarian principles are driving the new push for euthanasia.

Environmentalists continue to speak about the threat of overpopulation. Last week [March 20, 2009], Jonathon Porritt, a top "green" advisor to British Prime Minister Gordon Brown, called for cutting in half, from about 60 million people to about 30 million people, Great Britain's population, which, Porritt said, "is putting the world under terrible pressure. Each person in Britain has far more impact on the environment than those in developing countries so cutting our population is one way to reduce that impact."

An ambivalent public won't stop those determined to put us on the road to liberalized euthanasia laws and health-care rationing.

A handy way to cut down on the living is to kill off the ballooning population of elderly, who strain government-run health care schemes. Though physician-assisted suicide is officially outlawed in Britain, a recent report found that approximately 2,500 patients a year are given drugs that accelerate their death in what some are calling "euthanasia by the back door."

Last week, the British government announced that Parliament will consider a provision to allow suicide tourism, making it legal for Britons to travel to other countries to commit suicide.

In the United States, where 30 percent of Medicare spending pays for care in the final year of patients' lives, the euthanasia movement has an opportunity. The American public is ambivalent about the morality of doctor-assisted suicide. According to Gallup polling, between 2004 and 2007, the share of Americans who considered assisted suicide morally acceptable actually decreased from 53 to 49 percent, while the share that felt it was morally wrong increased from 41 to 44 percent.

But an ambivalent public won't stop those determined to put us on the road to liberalized euthanasia laws and health-care rationing. In recent years, a number of state legislatures have considered futile-care bills, which permit doctors to refuse treatment to patients even if it violates the patient's written advance directive.

Tucked inside the "there's no time to debate" stimulus bill was $1 billion for research into creating guidelines to direct doctors' treatment of difficult high cost medical problems. The provision establishes within the Department of Health and Human Services an Office of the National Coordinator for Health Information Technology, part of whose purpose is to "reduce health care costs resulting from inefficiency, medical errors, inappropriate care, duplicative care, and incomplete information." Soon Washington will have to agree that treatment you receive is cost-effective.

A Duty to Die

Recently, American Values President Gary Bauer and I argued that the abortion movement has undergone a philosophical shift, from being "pro-choice" to "pro-abortion." Policies enacted by President Obama and the Democratic-controlled Congress force all American taxpayers to underwrite abortion at home and abroad, and the repealing of conscience provisions will compel pro-life medical professionals to participate in abortion.

The debate surrounding doctor-assisted suicide is changing in the same way. Many of its advocates have moved beyond trying to secure "the right to die." Soon the burdensome will have a duty to die.

The Legalization of Assisted Suicide Does Not Lead to a Slippery Slope

Arthur Schafer

Arthur Schafer is a philosophy professor and the director of the Centre for Professional and Applied Ethics at the University of Manitoba in Canada.

Parliament [of Canada] will soon vote on a private member's bill to legalize euthanasia and physician-assisted suicide, subject to safeguards. And the Quebec College of Physicians has just endorsed euthanasia in some circumstances and is calling for Criminal Code amendments to protect doctors who hasten the death of suffering patients when those patients face "imminent and inevitable death."

If we decide to take time out from arguing over who should be first in line for the [2009 swine] flu vaccine, we might find our attention captured by this debate about ethics at the end of life.

When I began teaching ethics to undergraduate medical students in 1970, the hot-button issues were passive and indirect euthanasia. "Passive euthanasia" referred to the withholding or withdrawal of life support, from the motive of mercy, usually at the request of a dying patient. Doctors used to worry about both the ethics and the legality of hastening a patient's death by "pulling the plug."

"Indirect euthanasia" was the term then in use to describe the administration of large, sometimes very large, doses of analgesia with the direct aim of relieving pain but in the knowledge that, indirectly, this pain relief was likely to depress the patient's respiratory system and thereby bring on death more quickly.

Arthur Schafer, "The Great Canadian Euthanasia Debate," *Globe & Mail* (Toronto), November 6, 2009, p. A25. All rights reserved. Reproduced by permission.

"Passive euthanasia" is now called "appropriate care." Today, it is universally practised in Canadian hospitals, and no physician has been charged with a criminal offence for withholding or withdrawing life support, whether at the request of a dying patient, in compliance with a living will or at the request of the patient's family when the patient was no longer competent.

In 1992, Nancy B., a 25-year-old quadriplegic, told a Quebec Superior Court judge: "I am fed up with living on a respirator. It's no longer a life." The court ruled in her favour, and she was disconnected from life support. This case helped to establish that, in Canada, a competent adult has the right to refuse life-prolonging treatment.

Patients' wishes are better respected than previously and society has come to accept the importance of individual autonomy at the end of life.

"Indirect euthanasia" is now seen as merely a form of palliative care. A physician who denies adequate pain relief to a dying patient because of fears that the analgesic might cause death would be considered unprofessional. Today, many Canadian hospitals have palliative-care wards in which the overall treatment goal is to keep the patient comfortable rather than to prolong life. In these wards and in hospices for the dying, there is little hesitation in administering whatever dose of painkiller is required for comfort, even when the foreseeable consequence is hastened death.

An Increase in Respect for Individuals

One important lesson to be learned from these historical debates is that not all slopes are slippery. Opponents of so-called passive euthanasia balefully predicted that, if doctors were allowed to withhold or withdraw life support, we would immediately find ourselves on a slippery slope. Doctors who pulled the plug on dying patients would become desensitized or even brutalized. Hospitals would become cruel and dehumanized places. Patients would come to think of their doctors as executioners. The fundamental social value of respect for life would be debased. The elderly and the vulnerable would be at high risk of merciless killing.

But experience has shown that what happened was exactly the opposite of what was predicted by the naysayers: Doctors and hospitals have become kinder and gentler, patients' wishes are better respected than previously and society has come to accept the importance of individual autonomy at the end of life.

Let's consider where the euthanasia debate stands today. When palliative care doesn't provide needed relief from severe and intractable suffering, a growing number of hospitals now offer "sedation to unconsciousness": The patient is rendered terminally unconscious, and food and fluids are then discontinued. For many people, however, terminal sedation seems an undignified way to end one's life. Instead, they seek physician-assisted suicide.

The Need for Choice

Physician-assisted suicide has been legal in Oregon for 11 years and accounts for about one out of every thousand deaths a year. But, although it's not used often, one in six patients discusses this option with their family, and one in 50 raises it with their doctor. In other words, the safeguards appear to work. Few people opt for physician-assisted suicide, but many take comfort from the knowledge that, if their lives become unbearable, they can request—and be given—assistance to die.

Of course, as doctors sometimes acknowledge, euthanasia and assisted suicide are practised secretly in both the United States and Canada. Where these practices are illegal, they are practised in the dark and thus much more likely to result in mistakes and abuse.

Critics widely predicted that legalizing physician-assisted suicide would be a slippery slope to cutbacks in palliative care. Society would reason: Why offer expensive comfort care to suffering patients when it's cheaper to hasten their deaths? In practice, the opposite has occurred. Oregon legislation requires that dying patients be offered a full range of options, and the state has become a leader in palliative and end-of-life care.

Is it too much to hope that our legislators might learn from recent history? When it comes to end-of-life care, Canadians should be able to choose from among a full range of options, including first-rate palliative care and physician-assisted suicide. With proper safeguards in place to ensure openness and accountability, there's no reason to deny people the help they want and need.

Failing to Allow Assisted Suicide Results in Unnecessary Tragedies

Gary Cartwright

Gary Cartwright is a senior editor and feature writer for Texas Monthly *magazine.*

One night recently, during a dinner table conversation, an attractive, cultured, well-educated friend in her late sixties declared with surprising finality. "If I had stage-four pancreatic cancer. I'd put a revolver in my mouth and go night-night." She was reacting to a newspaper article we had all read about a 66-year-old woman in Sequim, Washington, who, in the final stages of a terminal illness, chose to die by way of doctor-assisted suicide, now legal thanks to the passage of a new state law. We all agreed that the Death With Dignity Act sounded better than a revolver in the mouth. The law passed last November [2008] with 58 percent of the vote, making Washington the second state, after Oregon, to legalize assisted suicide, which is a crime elsewhere in the United States and many parts of the world. (What's the punishment for assisting a suicide? Hanging?)

Death has become a curiously popular topic with many of my old friends, emphasis on "old." Aging has a way of redefining inevitability—of throwing into stark relief our right to die, something we had always taken for granted. If we believe in the right to life, shouldn't we likewise accept that people have a right to dispose of that life, regardless of health considerations, whenever and however they want? Apparently not. The pro-life movement rejects freedom of choice in all its insidious forms. This being the case, it becomes a contest of wits to see how we can subvert law and custom.

An Ancient Controversy

For as long as we've had politicians who believe it's their job to define and redefine what we can do with our own bodies, suicide, assisted suicide, attempted suicide, and euthanasia have been incredibly controversial acts responded to badly by the authorities. In ancient Athens, Plato believed that a person who committed "unacceptable" suicide without permission of the state—heaven forbid—should be buried without a headstone or marker on the outskirts of town. In France in 1670, a criminal ordinance fashioned by Louis XIV ordered that suicide victims be dragged facedown through the streets, after which they were thrown on garbage heaps. Beginning in 1879, people who attempted to kill themselves in England were sentenced to two years of hard labor. Legal views on taking one's life range from the absurd to the unspeakably cruel. In Pakistan, girls who are raped customarily kill themselves. Jews traditionally celebrate the mass suicide at Masada, even though Judaism forbids self-mutilation.

If we believe in the right to life, shouldn't we likewise accept that people have a right to dispose of that life, regardless of health considerations, whenever and however they want?

This summer [2009] in Austin, [Texas,] police and prosecutors stumbled and stammered as they searched for justice in the heartbreaking case of 52-year-old Kim Yarbrough. Kim was charged with murder—specifically, with causing the death of her 62-year-old invalid husband, Lloyd, by injecting his feeding tube with an assortment of prescription drugs, after which she unsuccessfully tried to take her own life. The ultimate nightmare isn't death; it's failing at death's door, waking up alive, and realizing your last best hope for peace is gone. Especially if you're handcuffed to the bed.

The story of Lloyd and Kim will move you to tears, unless you're someone who believes that only God has the right to end suffering. As detailed by reporter Andrea Ball, in the *Austin American-Statesman*: Lloyd and Kim met in the early nineties, dated for a time, then married in 1997. Lloyd had his own woodworking business. Kim worked in a gem store and was a competitive swimmer; they traveled together to swim meets. Life appeared good until 2004, when he was diagnosed with non-Hodgkin's lymphoma, a cancer that attacks the immune system. After extensive chemotherapy, radiation, and a bone marrow transplant, Lloyd's cancer seemed under control. But in the summer of 2007, he got encephalitis, a viral infection that causes the brain to swell, and he lapsed into a coma. When he woke, he couldn't walk or talk or swallow or go to the bathroom without help.

Depression and Despair

Kim placed Lloyd in a private rehabilitation center, but eventually their insurance ran out. She turned to Medicaid and moved him into a nursing home. Like most aging couples, they had talked about the indignity of dying in such a place. Lloyd had watched his mother waste away in a nursing home and had told Kim that he didn't want to end his life that way, so she brought him home and did the best she could. In her blog, Kim wrote of being overwhelmed by depression and despair. "I wonder if I will ever change Lloyd's diaper without feeling the pain of what has been lost," she wrote. In a later entry, she mused: "Everybody dies. Some people don't live all that long. It's not so tragic. Why should I try to keep living through all this?"

In May, in a quiet ceremony attended by a few close friends and neighbors, Lloyd and Kim renewed their wedding vows. She wore the same white, summery dress she had been married in twelve years earlier, and Lloyd was dressed in the same gold Hawaiian shirt. He sat in his wheelchair, of course, unable to walk or even say "I do." District judge Jon Wisser, who had presided over their original nuptials, said the words for him, and the guests repeated them. When Kim pledged her love, Lloyd kissed her hand and hugged her hips, his eyes flooding with tears. Three weeks later he was dead, and Kim was charged with murder. She is currently free on $20,000 bond.

The ultimate nightmare isn't death; it's failing at death's door, waking up alive, and realizing your last best hope for peace is gone.

In late July, two months after Lloyd's death, the Travis County district attorney's office was trying to figure out how to proceed. "It's an ongoing investigation," an assistant DA [district attorney] told me. On the advice of her attorney, Kim won't talk about the charges against her. I got the impression that no one wanted to prosecute her, but what to do about the law that makes what she did patently illegal? As things stand, the authorities have no wiggle room.

We often hear about people like Lloyd and Kim—ordinary people caught in the ordinary attrition of life, facing the pain and agony of death, trying to decide what to do. I've been in that situation a couple of times, first, when my son Mark died of leukemia, then again when Phyllis, my wife of nearly thirty years, died of lung cancer. Like most people, I did nothing. I simply waited for the end. In both instances, it came blessedly soon, but I will never forget the helplessness and loneliness of the wait or the mounting conviction that there had to be a better way, that we owed it to victims and survivors alike to provide options.

There are movements in a few states to legalize doctor-assisted suicide, but not in Texas, where the pro-life dogma is so powerful it's nearly killing us. I know the arguments against euthanasia: It devalues human life; it can too easily and inappropriately become a way of containing health care costs; physicians shouldn't be involved in directly causing someone's death. Some opponents fear a slippery slope effect—that a law intended to permit terminally ill patients a way to die in peace can become a handy escape route for people who are merely depressed or momentarily ticked off. Most of these arguments are specious. Though it is perfectly rational to want to avoid the pain and suffering of a terminal illness, the act itself nearly always seems irrational from the outside. One of the strangest double suicides on record took place this summer in the North Texas town of Henrietta, which has been in shock since a disastrous prairie fire destroyed the neighboring town of Ringgold three years ago. In the aftermath of the fire, the Reverend Eldon Earl Johnson and his wife, Linda Kay Johnson, were steadfast and strong, ministering to their flock and helping rebuild the Ringgold Baptist Church, which sustained smoke damage. Then, at the very moment when everyone should have been celebrating life, the Johnsons walked to the railroad tracks and calmly prepared to be hit by a train.

The Arrogance of the Law

Surely we can do better. We could start by thinking of death as a commodity—something you might trade on the stock exchange, like pork bellies. A Swiss lawyer named Ludwig Minelli founded the suicide-facilitating organization Dignitas, which is headquartered in Zurich, and plans to open other clinics where people who are terminally ill or have severe physical illnesses can lie down in a comfortable room and sip a lethal cocktail of barbiturates. (One anti-euthanasia advocate has termed it "sort of a Starbucks for suicide.")

Minelli's clinic got international attention recently when one of Britain's most celebrated cultural figures, Sir Edward Downes, flew to Zurich and checked in with his wife. Lady

Joan Downes, a 74-year-old former choreographer, ballet dancer, and television producer, was in the final stages of terminal cancer. The 85-year-old Sir Edward, once the principal conductor of the BBC Philharmonic Orchestra and also the associate music director of the Royal Opera House, at Covent Garden, in London, wasn't terminally ill, but he was nearly blind and deaf. The couple's children watched in tears as their parents drank a small amount of clear liquid, then lay down on adjacent beds, holding hands. "Within a couple of minutes they were asleep, and they died within ten minutes," reported their son, Caractacus Downes. "They wanted to be next to each other when they died." They had spent 54 years together and decided to end their lives when and where they desired, rather than struggle helplessly to the same inevitable result. "It is a very civilized way to end your life," Caractacus said. "I don't understand why the legal position in [the U.K.] doesn't allow it."

Though it is perfectly rational to want to avoid the pain and suffering of a terminal illness, the act itself nearly always seems irrational from the outside.

Scotland Yard says it's "looking into the circumstances" of the deaths of Sir Edward and Lady Joan. How predictably officious. How stupidly arrogant. How disappointingly reminiscent of the attitude of lawmakers and law enforcers in Texas and elsewhere. Are they so obtuse that they don't understand that this shouldn't be their call? Maybe we should explain it in simple terms, as we would to a child: Be patient, my little ones. Your time will come.

CHAPTER 4

Does Assisted Suicide Work Well Where It Is Legal?

Overview: Legal Assisted Suicide in the United States

Brad Knickerbocker

Brad Knickerbocker is a staff writer for The Christian Science Monitor.

In a move that is both ethically profound and (so far, at least) politically rare, Montana has become the third state to legalize physician-assisted suicide.

A divided state supreme court ruled Thursday [December 31, 2009,] that neither state law nor public policy prevented doctors from prescribing lethal drugs to terminally-ill patients who want to end their lives.

In essence, the court ruled, suicide is not a crime. The majority justices wrote:

> "We find nothing in Montana Supreme Court precedent or Montana statutes indicating that physician aid in dying is against public policy. The 'against public policy' exception to consent has been interpreted by this court as applicable to violent breaches of the public peace. Physician aid in dying does not satisfy that definition. We also find nothing in the plain language of Montana statutes indicating that physician aid in dying is against public policy. In physician aid in dying, the patient—not the physician—commits the final death-causing act by self-administering a lethal dose of medicine."

The ruling—which is likely to be challenged in the legislature and perhaps in a voter referendum—follows a pattern in the Pacific Northwest.

In November 2008, voters in Washington State approved a ballot initiative allowing terminally ill, legally competent adults to obtain lethal prescriptions without exposing themselves or their doctors to criminal prosecution. The Washington measure was modeled on Oregon's Death with Dignity Act enacted in 1997 following voter approval and upheld by the US Supreme Court in 2006.

Montana has become the third state to legalize physician-assisted suicide.

The Oregon law strictly prohibits "lethal injection, mercy killing, or active euthanasia." But it allows mentally competent adults who declare their intentions in writing, and have been diagnosed as terminally ill, to take a doctor-prescribed lethal drug themselves, orally, after a waiting period.

Since the law went into effect in 1998, about 40 people a year have taken their own life this way. Last year, 60 individuals did so (out of 88 who received the prescriptions).

Over the years, there have been no reported violations under the law—no evidence that individuals have been pressured by doctors or family members. And Oregon has become noted for the quality of end-of-life care, especially the use of hospices.

Missoula attorney Mark Connell, who represented plaintiff physicians and patients, described the decision as "a victory for individual rights over government control."

"The Montana Supreme Court has now recognized that, where intensely personal and private choices regarding end-of-life care are involved, Montana law entrusts those decisions to the individuals whose lives are at stake, not the government," he said in a statement released by Compassion & Choices, the main group lobbying in favor of physician-assisted suicide.

Pro-life groups took a different view.

Jeff Laszloffy of the Montana Family Foundation told Life-News.com, "Definitely not what we wanted, but not as bad as it could have been."

Changing the Law

"What the court did, in essence, was to place the issue back into the hands of the legislature, where it should be," Mr. Laszloffy said. "They said there's nothing currently in statute that prohibits the practice. It's now up to us to go into the next legislative session fully armed and ready to pass statutory language that says, once and for all, that physician assisted suicide is illegal in Montana."

Assisted Suicide Works Well in Oregon

Kathryn L. Tucker

Kathryn L. Tucker is director of legal affairs for Compassion &
Choices, a nonprofit organization whose mission is to improve
care and expand choice at the end of life.

The Oregon Death with Dignity Act demonstrates that aid-
in-dying laws can, and do, work well. The Dignity Act es-
tablishes tightly controlled procedures under which competent, terminally ill adults who are under the care of an
attending physician may obtain a prescription for medication
to allow them to control the time, place, and manner of their
own impending death. The attending physician must, among
other things, determine that the patient is mentally competent
and an Oregon resident, and confirm the patient's diagnosis
and prognosis. To qualify as "terminally ill," a person must
have "an incurable and irreversible disease that has been medically confirmed and will, within reasonable medical judgment,
produce death within six months."

The Death with Dignity Act

The attending physician must also inform persons requesting
such medication of their diagnosis and prognosis, the risks
and probable results of taking the medication, and alternatives
to taking their own lives, including—although not limited
to—hospice care and pain relief. A consulting physician must
confirm the attending physician's medical opinion.

Once a request from a qualifying patient has been properly documented and witnessed, and all waiting periods have
expired, the attending physician may prescribe, but not ad-

Kathryn L. Tucker, "In the Laboratory of the States: The Progress of *Glucksberg's* Invita-
tion to States to Address End-of-Life Choice," *Michigan Law Review*, vol. 106, no. 8, June
2009, pp. 1593–1611. All rights reserved. Reproduced by permission.

minister, medication to enable the patient to end his or her life in a humane and dignified manner. The Dignity Act protects physicians and pharmacists who act in compliance with its comprehensive procedures from civil or criminal sanctions and any professional disciplinary actions based on that conduct.

The Oregon Death with Dignity Act demonstrates that aid-in-dying laws can, and do, work well.

The Dignity Act requires healthcare providers to file reports with the state documenting their actions. Oregon's experience with aid in dying has therefore been extensively documented and studied. To date, the Oregon Public Health Division and Department of Human Services have issued nine annual reports that present and evaluate the state's experience with the Dignity Act. Related reports and articles have also been published in leading medical journals. These reports constitute the only source of reliable data regarding actual experience with legal, regulated physician-assisted dying in America. . . .

No Evidence of Risk to Patients

The experience in Oregon has demonstrated that a carefully drafted law does not place patients at risk. In a report examining the Oregon experience to assess whether vulnerable populations were put at risk, the researchers concluded that there was no evidence supporting this concern. The Oregon experience has caused even staunch opponents to admit that continued opposition to such a law can only be based on personal, moral, or religious grounds.

The Oregon reports have shown the dire predictions of those initially opposed to the Dignity Act to have been unfounded. The data demonstrate that the option of physician-assisted dying has not been unwillingly forced upon those who are poor, uneducated, uninsured, or otherwise disadvantaged. In fact, the studies show just the opposite. For example, the eighth annual report found that a higher level of education is strongly associated with the use of physician-assisted dying; those with a baccalaureate degree or higher were 7.9 times more likely than those without a high school diploma to choose physician-assisted dying. The report found that 100% of patients opting for physician-assisted dying under the Dignity Act had either private health insurance, Medicare, or Medicaid, and 92% were enrolled in hospice care. Furthermore, the reports demonstrate that use of physician-assisted dying is limited. During the first nine years in which physician-assisted dying was a legal option, only 292 Oregonians chose it. And although there has been a gradual increase in the rate of those opting for physician-assisted dying, the overall rate remains low: the 38 terminally ill adults who chose this option in 2005 represented only 12 deaths for every 10,000 Oregonians who died that year. A 2000 survey of Oregon physicians found that they granted 1 in 6 requests for aid in dying, and that only 1 in 10 requests resulted in hastened death. Roughly one-third of those patients who complete the process of seeking medications under the Dignity Act do not go on to consume the medications. These individuals derive comfort from having the option to control the time of death yet ultimately die of their disease without exercising that control.

Outside Observers

Outside observers, after carefully studying implementation of the aid-in-dying law in Oregon, have concluded that the law poses no risk to patients. For example, a report prepared for the Vermont legislature, after thoroughly reviewing the Oregon experience, concluded that "it is quiet [sic] apparent from credible sources in and out of Oregon that the Death with Dignity Act has not had an adverse impact on end-of-life care and in all probability has enhanced the other options." Leading scholars have come to conclusions such as this: "I worried about people being pressured to do this. . . . But this data confirms . . . that the policy in Oregon is working. There is no evidence of abuse or coercion, or misuse of the policy."

Indeed, rather than posing a risk to patients or the medical profession, the Dignity Act has galvanized significant improvements in the care of the dying in Oregon. Oregon doctors report that since the passage of the Dignity Act, efforts have been made to improve their ability to provide adequate end-of-life care. These efforts include improving their knowledge of the use of pain medications for the terminally ill, improving their ability to recognize depression and other psychiatric disorders, and more frequently referring their patients to hospice programs. One survey of Oregon physicians on their efforts to improve end-of-life care since 1994 found that 30% of respondents increased their number of referrals to hospice care and 76% made efforts to increase their knowledge of pain medication. A survey of hospice nurses and social workers in Oregon reveals that they observed, during a period from 1998 to 2003, an increase in physicians' knowledge of palliative care and willingness both to refer and to care for hospice patients.

Data confirms . . . that the policy in Oregon is working. There is no evidence of abuse or coercion, or misuse of the policy.

In addition to the improvement of end-of-life care, the legal option of aid in dying has psychological benefits for both the terminally ill and the healthy. The availability of the option of aid in dying gives the terminally ill autonomy, control, and choice, which physicians in Oregon have identified as the overwhelming motivational factor behind the decision to request assistance in dying. Healthy Oregonians know that if they ever face a terminal illness, they will have control and choice over their manner of death.

The data demonstrate that, far from posing any hazard to patients or the practice of medicine, making the option of assisted dying available has galvanized improvements in end-of-life care and benefited all terminally ill Oregonians. A central argument against allowing patients access to aid in dying has been that risks would arise if the option were available. Actual experience demonstrates that these risks do not, in fact, exist. And the lack of these risks undermines the argument against aid in dying. This has led some major medical organizations to conclude that passage of Oregon-type aid-in-dying laws is good policy and to adopt policy supporting passage of such laws.

Legal Assisted Suicide in Oregon Has Led to Improved Palliative Care

Courtney S. Campbell

Courtney S. Campbell is the Hundere Professor in Religion and Culture in the Philosophy Department at Oregon State University.

The Oregon Death with Dignity Act (ODDA), which permits physicians to write a prescription for lethal drugs to qualified terminally ill patients, has been in effect for a little over a decade. It has, from October 1997 to the present, been the only such statute in the United States permitting what is variously called "physician-assisted suicide," "physician aid in dying," or "death with dignity" (the statute refers to the procedure as the ending of life in a "humane and dignified manner"). . . .

Death with dignity is the death of choice for relatively few persons. Before the act was implemented, opponents anticipated a demographic migration of near-terminal patients to Oregon, such that Oregon would become a "suicide center" for the terminally ill, with all sorts of ensuing social catastrophes. The empirical evidence does not bear out these projections. In ten years, 541 Oregon residents have received lethal prescriptions to end their lives; of this number, 341 patients actually ingested the drugs. These figures are not only lower than the substantial numbers predicted by opponents, they are even smaller than the more conservative estimates anticipated by advocates. While those figures have generally risen each year, the deaths under the ODDA still comprise a very low proportion of Oregon's total deaths.

Courtney S. Campbell, "Ten Years of 'Death with Dignity,'" *New Atlantis*, no. 22, Fall 2008. All rights reserved. Reproduced by permission.

Given the predictions of both the ODDA's original supporters and opponents, one might be inclined to ask not why are some terminally ill patients seeking recourse to physician-assisted suicide, but rather why aren't *more* of them doing so? In some years, and in some cases, the prospect of federal intervention may have had a kind of "chilling" effect—if not necessarily among patients requesting such assistance, then on willing physician participants. There may also be a general demographic factor at work: younger persons may be more willing to support physician-assisted suicide than elderly persons who may be staring their own mortality, or that of loved ones, in the face.

However, a likelier explanation may be that the ODDA served as a catalyst to improved end-of-life care among Oregon practitioners—including the increased use of hospice and palliative care, and the easing of restrictions on the drugs practitioners could provide to relieve pain. This is a very significant possibility, because it implies that ensuring a dignified death may not be a matter of changing the laws so much as a matter of changing medical practices and professional education. Moreover, it suggests that, for most people, a pharmacologically-induced death is not a precondition of a dignified death, nor that the possession of a right entails its subsequent use.

The Situation in Other States

Other states have not followed the Oregon model. In the months following its passage in November 1994, the ODDA was heralded as a national model for other states in addressing issues presented by terminally ill patients, particularly as it went beyond the traditional moral and legal boundary of treatment refusal but stopped short of an even more controversial practice, physician-administered euthanasia. Yet, despite numerous efforts—including in state legislatures and by citizen initiatives—Oregon has been more the national maverick than the national model. Although the I-1000 initiative is likely to be approved in Washington [and was passed in 2008], the interesting question is why other states have not followed the path that Oregon thought itself to be pioneering.

---

the [Oregon Death with Dignity Act] served as a catalyst to improved end-of-life care among Oregon practitioners—including the increased use of hospice and palliative care.

For one reason or another, an act like Oregon's may not be necessary or feasible for many states. First, although suicide has been decriminalized and euthanasia remains a form of homicide in all states, the legal situation is not so clear-cut when it comes to statutes on physician assistance in suicide. Some states do not have specific laws prohibiting physician-assisted suicide; among states that do have such laws, violations may not be reported, the laws may not be enforced, or the participating provider may not be convicted or sentenced. That is to say, substantial discretion and flexibility on these questions are already embedded in the laws of many states. If we understand law to be not simply a social mechanism for restraining wrongdoing but also an educator of social values, it may be that the mere possibility of passing such an act serves as sufficient impetus to find alternatives for improving care at the end of life.

The Rationale of Patients Who Use ODDA

Patients seem relatively free of or immune from coercive influences. In the run-up to its passage, a significant objection to the ODDA was that even though its advocates were using the rhetoric of patient choice and self-determination, patient choices would ultimately reflect compromised voluntariness or even coercion. Put another way, though the act sought to legalize one method for exercising a "right to die," critics were concerned that patients could subjectively experience this as a "*duty* to die" for the benefit of family or others.

This perception was reinforced by various studies of physicians' attitudes towards patient choices. For example, a 1996 study (conducted while the act was being legally contested and published in the *New England Journal of Medicine*) reported that more than 93 percent of 2,761 polled Oregon physicians believed a patient might request lethal drugs "because of concern about being a burden," and more than 83 percent believed a patient may make such a request "because of financial pressure." If these were the motivating factors in patient decisions, contrary to the stated rationale of expanding patient choice and rights, the ODDA could be seen as limiting choice or coercing decisions.

Patients seem relatively free of or immune from coercive influences.

In practice, according to the ODDA data collected by the Oregon government, becoming a "burden" to family and other caregivers emerged as an end-of-life concern for 39 percent of the 341 patients who have used the act in its first decade—a not insignificant number, but still much lower than the percentage of patients who expressed direct self-regarding concerns about loss of autonomy, diminished quality of life, loss of dignity, and loss of control of bodily functions. Less than 3 percent expressed concerns about the financial implications of treatment.

A caveat is necessary here: The demographic information collected by the Oregon Department of Human Services involves reports only from *physicians* about patient concerns—so the information is second-hand and may not penetrate to the depth of patient motivations that a firsthand qualitative interview might. Moreover, the information compiled from physician reports is generated by a government-issued standardized form that asks the physician to mark any of seven boxes that best reflect the reporting physician's view of the concerns contributing to the patient's request for a lethal drug—forcing physicians to use generic categories that may imperfectly, if at all, express their patients' subjective experiences and motivations. Because of these limitations in the state-sanctioned reporting method, other studies have attempted to more accurately identify the reasons for patient choices. For example, a 2003 study published in the *Journal of Palliative Medicine* fastened more on patient concerns over "control of the dying process" that had been relayed to physicians, a concept that is intimated but not specifically described in the seven categories on the state reporting form. It is also unfortunate that no empirical research has been conducted on the reasons why most eligible terminally ill patients have said "no," either explicitly or implicitly by their actions, when it comes to exercising their right to request a lethal prescription.

These considerations notwithstanding, the procedures embedded in the statute for ensuring informed and voluntary decisions by terminally ill patients have been substantially effective. The pre-implementation concerns of critics about coerced or compromised choices do not seem borne out in practice.

Normalizing Dignified Dying

"Death with dignity" has been largely normalized in medical practice and moral discourse. The passage of the ODDA in 1994 and its decade of implementation without the dire consequences envisioned by opponents has altered the tenor of discourse about ethical options at the end of life. The question is no longer *whether* physician-assisted suicide should be permitted within medicine, but *how* to regulate and monitor the approved processes effectively. Instead of grappling with the fundamental moral questions, commentary about the act now often sticks to the far more mundane questions of over-

sight and administration. Physician-assisted suicide, no longer novel, doesn't possess the sharp edge it once had in public, professional, and bioethical debate; it has largely been supplanted by more hot-button issues, such as research on embryonic stem cells or new genetic breakthroughs.

While college students are not the truest gauge of the cultural *Zeitgeist*, it has been remarkable to me to observe the shift in student attitudes at my state university from 1994 to the present. Prior to its passage, students in biomedical ethics courses considered the ODDA a "burning issue," a "hot topic," one that made for a good debate, and a subject for which there were commonly significant differences in opinion. And student engagement with the issue, as evidenced by the number of related term papers, ran broad and deep. By contrast, today's students, ten years after the ODDA's implementation, have been acculturated to a "right to death with dignity" as just "the way things are." They find it difficult to see the issue as morally or professionally relevant, and they commonly wonder what "the problem" is with the other forty-nine states, and why, after more than ten years, Oregon is still the only state with such a law. Student engagement through submitted term papers has declined from nearly 30 percent of students to approximately 3 percent. In my most recent class, not a single student raised an objection to Washington I-1000.

The passage of the [Oregon Death with Dignity Act] led to a greater effort on the part of physicians and palliative and hospice care teams to ensure adequate pain control.

Some implications of the ODDA's implementation were easier to foresee, including the general improvement of pain control, the overall lack of medical complications resulting from the lethal drug, and an ongoing confusion about how the act works in practice.

Palliative care and pain control emerged as a paramount focus of end-of-life care. As described above, the supporters of the ODDA in the 1990s often invoked "hard cases"—nightmarish scenarios of terminally ill patients tortured by unrelenting pain. This rhetoric was intended to evoke public sympathies towards the plight of persons whose condition made them very vulnerable, as well as dismay—if not outrage—at the apparent indifference in the medical system, religious communities, and the law towards such patients. The implication was that these patients were destined to live out their final days either tethered to technological life support (and perhaps unconscious) or in substantial pain, unless the ODDA became law and professional compassion joined with respect to enable a hastened death.

Ensuring Adequate Pain Control

In fact, the passage of the ODDA led to a greater effort on the part of physicians and palliative and hospice care teams to ensure adequate pain control. A Task Force to Improve the Care of Terminally-Ill Oregonians was established to bring greater awareness to the question of pain management immediately following implementation. The task force issued an influential report in 1998 that practitioners still rely on a decade later. Institutions involved in pain management developed new protocols, and laws that had raised the prospect of licensure investigations of physicians who provided more pain medication than called for in conventional medical protocols were rescinded. Thus, physicians no longer faced a professional and legal deterrent against the use of personalized pain control methods.

As noted above, the lower-than-expected number of patients requesting lethal drugs can likely be attributed in part to these improvements in the quality of pain management. And even the patients who requested and used lethal prescriptions—recall, 27 percent of those 341 patients said they were worried about inadequate pain control—may not have been *experiencing* pain in their terminal phase but rather *anticipating* and hoping to avoid a painful death.

Medical Complications of the Lethal Drugs

The lethal drugs are largely without additional medical complications. A central argument of opponents of the ODDA was that through the prescribed drugs, physicians would be exposing their patients to substantial risks of harm, including severe complications, lingering deaths, and unintentionally induced comas. This claim was emphasized because there was (understandably) no reliable body of medical evidence on what drugs and dose ranges would bring about a patient's death without complications. Thus, it was argued, rather than benefiting the patient by providing the means to a hastened death, the patients would risk continued life in a "worse-than-death" condition—in which case the prospect of euthanasia, which was a violation of the statute, would be necessary to end life.

This fear seemed overstated at the time, drawing as it did on disputed anecdotal accounts from the Dutch experience with physician-assisted suicide and physician-administered euthanasia. Indeed, the implementation of the ODDA indicates that those concerns were unfounded. According to the physician reporting system, almost 95 percent of patients have experienced no complications; just over 5 percent of patients have initially regurgitated the lethal dose. There have been no interventions by emergency medical services, and the time frame between ingestion of the prescription and death has ranged from as short as one minute to as long as three and a half days, with the median being 25 minutes. It would be useful to know the minimal and maximal time frames beyond which a patient can be said to have experienced "complications," because disclosure of such information is necessary to any authentic process of informed consent—but unfortunately the state reporting system does not assess this.

In this regard, it is also important to ask *who* would determine if complications of one sort or another had been experienced by the patient. In only 28 percent of the patient deaths has the prescribing physician been present at the time of patient ingestion of the lethal dose, and in 19 percent of the cases, no health care provider has been in attendance. In the remaining 53 percent of patient deaths, some provider besides the prescribing physician has been present at the time of ingestion.

Despite all the legal and educational efforts seeking to inform Oregon residents of their rights and options pertaining to end-of-life choices, there remains a good deal of confusion.

The case for physician-assisted suicide as a safe and effective procedure with minimal complications would be strengthened if the prescribing physician, or at least the reporting physician, was present at both the time of ingestion and the time when death was declared. If the median time frame from ingestion to death is 25 minutes, it seems not too much to ask a professional to be present with the patient. Even if there are no complications, it would still be a profound gesture of presence and commitment to remain with the patient to the very end. And in circumstances where the actual time frame is not 25 minutes, but pushing 25 hours, or even 83 hours, continued monitoring by the professional would seem to be a necessary element of care.

Citizens can be confused about their rights and options regarding end-of-life choices. Despite all the legal and educational efforts seeking to inform Oregon residents of their rights and options pertaining to end-of-life choices, there remains a good deal of confusion, at least as expressed in public gatherings and discussion forums.

The state has two forms of advance directives, which can be used independently or in conjunction with each other, and which are comprehensive with respect to termination of medical treatment or appointment of a proxy. However, these advance directives are separate from the ODDA application process: terminally ill persons seeking lethal drugs must use an additional request form specific to the provisions of the act. An advance directive that includes a request for physician assistance in dying is unlikely to be honored. This is a point on which there seems to be significant confusion. Although there seems to be broad public consensus that certain kinds of death can be degrading and demeaning to dignity, and most people seem to want to avoid a persistent vegetative condition or a Terri Schiavo-like death, it is not clear in the minds of many citizens that the advance directive process that would apply in those circumstances is *separate* from the physician-assisted suicide process. There remains a compelling need for public education.

Non-Consequentialist Concerns

When the Oregon Death with Dignity Act first passed, it was heralded by some commentators as a "bold experiment." The first decade of that experiment's results are in: it seems that the practice of prescribing lethal drugs to terminally ill patients is effective and generally without further medical complications. Consequentialist objections to the act have largely been refuted by experience. Insofar as objections continue to be voiced by various advocacy groups or medical practitioners, they tend to rely on non-consequentialist appeals to the intrinsic value or sanctity of human life, or to the moral vocation of health care professionals. . . .

A brief personal assessment in conclusion: I have argued in the past that the Oregon Death with Dignity Act was a moral mistake. I have never agreed with the objections based on consequentialist catastrophes, but rather my opposition stemmed from a moral framework that permits the taking of human life—whether that be in self-defense, capital punishment, war, or end-of-life care—only as a last resort, and it has not seemed that society, or the state of Oregon specifically, had exhausted all alternatives—including better pain control, more and earlier referrals to hospice care, and effective education on advance directives—to achieve the goals of end-of-life care such that the last resort condition was satisfied. After a decade of living in a state where physician-assisted suicide has gradually reached the point of eliciting a "ho-hum" in the newspaper, I find myself still affirming that there are other ethically preferable policies to achieve patient choice, control, and "dignity" in the end of life, even while recognizing that individual patients do sometimes find themselves confronted with the need to employ that "last resort."

Assisted Suicide in Oregon Does Not Have Adequate Safeguards

Oregon Right to Life

Oregon Right to Life is an affiliate of the National Right to Life Committee, a pro-life organization.

Physician-assisted suicide involves a physician prescribing lethal drugs for a patient with the knowledge that the patient intends to use the drugs to commit suicide. Refusing a ventilator, or some other life sustaining machine or treatment is not assisted suicide and is legal. The intent of refusing medical treatment is not to end life, but to allow nature to take its course. With physician-assisted suicide the intent is to kill the patient.

Supporters of assisted suicide have long maintained that assisted suicide is necessary for those suffering from intractable pain; however, to date, there still is no documented case of assisted suicide being needed for untreatable pain. In fact, *in the list of reasons patients choose to use assisted suicide, pain, or fear of pain is the least used reason!* Dr. Linda Ganzini, professor of psychiatry at Oregon Health & Science University, surveyed family members of Oregon patients who requested assisted suicide. Her published report emphasizes this truth: "No physical symptoms experienced at the time of the request were rated higher than 2 on a 1 to 5 scale. In most cases, future concerns about physical symptoms were rated as more important than physical symptoms present at the time of the request." The study found that many physicians are surprised at the lack of suffering experienced by a patient who is requesting assisted suicide.

National studies show that among patients requesting assisted suicide, depression is the only factor that significantly predicts the request for death. An estimated 90% of suicides in the U.S. are associated with mental illness, most commonly depression. Diagnosing depression can be challenging, but is often found with good psychiatric care. In spite of these facts, in Oregon's 10th year, not even one suicide victim received psychiatric counseling.

Ganzini's study also confirmed what has been seen in publicized cases of physician assisted suicide: instead of patients having their fears and concerns addressed by physicians, once the request for assisted suicide is made, other care options are abandoned. The majority of physicians will not participate in assisted suicide. When these physicians refuse to assist in killing their patients, the patient will often then seek the help of assisted suicide proponents. These proponents shepherd patients to doctors who will write lethal prescriptions for patients they have just met. Many patients would change their minds about assisted suicide if interventions were made to help them maintain control, independence, and self-care, all in their home environment.

Physician-Assisted Suicide in America

On November 8, 1994, Oregon became the first government in the world to legalize physician-assisted suicide when voters passed a statewide ballot measure. After a lengthy court battle and the failure of a 1997 ballot measure to repeal the law, Oregon's assisted suicide law became functional in November, 1997. That year Oregon became the first jurisdiction in the world to begin experimenting with legalized assisted suicide.

Since the passage of Oregon's physician-assisted suicide law, many states have attempted to pass similar laws. Maine and Michigan voters rejected statewide ballot measures to legalize assisted suicide in their states. Legislators in Hawaii, Vermont, California, and other states, have rejected bills to legalize assisted suicide. Courts in Florida and Alaska turned back lawsuits from patients demanding they be given a right to physician-assisted suicide.

No oversight exists to insure patients are safeguarded from negligence or abuses of the law.

In the 1997 Supreme Court case, *Washington v. Glucksberg,* physician-assisted suicide was rejected as a constitutional right when the Court upheld both the New York and Washington statutes prohibiting assisted suicide by a 9-0 vote. Physician-assisted suicide is not a right protected by the U.S. Constitution.

The main concern about physician-assisted suicide is the inability to create safeguards or contain assisted suicide to any boundaries. Since legalizing assisted suicide, Oregonians have seen first-hand what really happens. When physician-assisted suicide is legalized, Oregonians have found out that safeguards don't work.

A shroud of secrecy encompasses the reporting process of assisted suicide. The Oregon Department of Health's annual report publishes raw statistics and no inquiry is held to verify even the most rudimentary of figures. No oversight exists to insure patients are safeguarded from negligence or abuses of the law. However publicized assisted suicide cases have proven:

- "Doctor shopping" is common. A network of assisted suicide proponents insure that patients will receive assisted suicide, even when their family doctor knows their desire for death could be alleviated.

- Familial pressure is applied on patients to commit assisted suicide.

- Patients suffering from depression and dementia are receiving physician-assisted suicide.

- Once receiving a drug overdose prescription from a pro-assisted suicide doctor, patients no longer receive concerned medical care, but instead are abandoned to die.

- While some pain-relieving and life-saving medications are not paid for by Oregon's Health Plan, assisted suicide is. In rejecting payment for these medications, the Health Department informs patients about the availability of assisted suicide.

Assisted Suicide in the Netherlands Has Expanded to Active Euthanasia

Disability Rights Education & Defense Fund

Disability Rights Education & Defense Fund is a national disability rights law and policy center that advances the civil and human rights of people with disabilities.

Most assisted suicide supporters claim that assisted suicide will be narrowly limited to people who are terminally ill, but these so-called "narrow" proposals, if enacted, can easily expand. As the New York State Task Force on Life and the Law wrote,

> Once society authorizes assisted suicide for . . . terminally ill patients experiencing unrelievable suffering, it will be difficult if not impossible to contain the option to such a limited group. Individuals who are not [able to make the choice for themselves], who are not terminally ill, or who cannot self-administer lethal drugs will also seek the option of assisted suicide, and no principled basis will exist to deny [it].

The example of the Netherlands demonstrates clearly that assisted suicide cannot be limited to a small, targeted group once Pandora's box is opened. The Dutch example provides the longest experience with assisted suicide in any country. Although it remained technically illegal until 2002, the Netherlands first began to legally tolerate assisted suicide in the early 70s. Today, active euthanasia—doctors giving lethal injections—has almost completely replaced assisted suicide.

The Netherlands has become a frightening laboratory experiment because of how far assisted suicide and lethal injections have spread. Herbert Hendin documented how assisted suicide and lethal injections have become not the rare exception, but the rule for people with terminal illness in the Netherlands. Hendin was one of only three foreign observers given the opportunity to study these medical practices in the Netherlands in depth, to discuss specific cases with leading practitioners, and to interview Dutch government-sponsored euthanasia researchers.

Hendin stated in Congressional testimony,

> Over the past two decades, the Netherlands has moved from assisted suicide to euthanasia, from euthanasia for the terminally ill to euthanasia for the chronically ill, from euthanasia for physical illness to euthanasia for psychological distress and from voluntary euthanasia to nonvoluntary and involuntary euthanasia. Once the Dutch accepted assisted suicide it was not possible legally or morally to deny more active medical [assistance to die], i.e. euthanasia, to those who could not effect their own deaths. Nor could they deny assisted suicide or euthanasia to the chronically ill who have longer to suffer than the terminally ill or to those who have psychological pain not associated with physical disease. To do so would be a form of discrimination. Involuntary euthanasia has been justified as necessitated by the need to make decisions for patients not [medically] competent to choose for themselves.

The example of the Netherlands demonstrates clearly that assisted suicide cannot be limited to a small, targeted group once Pandora's box is opened.

Hendin has also described how the government-sanctioned studies suggest an erosion of medical standards in the care of terminally ill patients in the Netherlands: 50 percent of Dutch cases of assisted suicide and euthanasia are not reported, more than 50 percent of Dutch doctors feel free to suggest euthanasia to their patients, and 25 percent of these doctors admit to ending patients' lives without their consent. Further, he reported that for a thousand people each year in the Netherlands, physicians have ended their patients' lives without consulting the patients.

U.S. assisted suicide advocates, attempting to distinguish the Oregon experience from that of the Netherlands, argue that the numbers of reported users of assisted suicide in Oregon are low. But in fact, the number of people requesting lethal drugs has steadily increased. In the beginning, the numbers were low in the Netherlands as well, but usage grew along with social acceptance of the practice. There is no reason to believe that legalization in the U.S. would not be followed, in 20 years or more, with the kind of extraordinary growth that has taken place in the Netherlands.

Lethal Drugs Often Ineffective

Assisted suicide proponents and medical personnel alike have established that taking lethal drugs by mouth is often ineffective in causing a quick and simple death. The body sometimes expels the drugs through vomiting, or the person falls into a lengthy state of unconsciousness rather than dying promptly, as assisted suicide advocates wish. Such ineffective suicide attempts happen in a substantial percentage of cases—estimates range from 15 percent to 25 percent. The way to prevent these "problems," in the view of euthanasia advocates, is by legalizing lethal injections by physicians—that is, legalizing active euthanasia. This is the likely next step if society first accepts assisted suicide as a legitimate legal option.

Assisted suicide proponents tell us that none of these things will happen in the United States. But once assisted suicide is legalized, no significant barriers remain to prevent them. The very existence of assisted suicide as a legal option is likely to gradually erode social resistance, as it has in the Netherlands. In fact, the leading public champion for assisted suicide in Washington State, former Governor Booth Gardner, openly articulated a vision of its expansion as his dream. According to the *New York Times Magazine* in December 2007:

> Gardner wants a law that would permit lethal prescriptions for people whose suffering is unbearable, a standard that can seem no standard at all; a standard that prevails in the Netherlands, the Western nation that has been boldest about legalizing aid in dying; a standard that elevates subjective experience over objective appraisal and that could engage the government and the medical profession in the administration of widespread suicide....
>
> Gardner's campaign is a compromise; he sees it as a first step. If he can sway Washington to embrace a restrictive law, then other states will follow. And gradually, he says, the nation's resistance will subside, the culture will shift and laws with more latitude will be passed.

Thus, the danger of expansion is another reason why it is important to maintain the legal barriers prohibiting assisted suicide.

Organizations to Contact

The editors have compiled the following list of organizations concerned with the issues debated in this book. The descriptions are derived from materials provided by the organizations. All have publications or information available for interested readers. The list was compiled on the date of publication of the present volume; names, addresses, phone and fax numbers, and e-mail and Internet addresses may change. Be aware that many organizations take several weeks or longer to respond to inquiries, so allow as much time as possible.

American Life League (ALL)
PO Box 1350, Stafford, VA   22555
(540) 659-4171 • fax: (540) 659-2586
website: www.all.org

The American Life League is a Roman Catholic pro-life organization committed to the protection of all innocent human beings from the moment of creation to natural death. ALL sponsors a number of outreach efforts opposing birth control, abortion, stem cell research, and euthanasia. ALL provides brochures, videos, and newsletters at its website, including the brochure *Euthanasia & You.*

American Society of Law, Medicine & Ethics (ASLME)
765 Commonwealth Ave., Ste. 1634, Boston, MA   02215
(617) 262-4990 • fax: (617) 437-7596
e-mail: info@aslme.org
website: www.aslme.org

The American Society of Law, Medicine & Ethics is a nonprofit educational organization focused on the intersection of law, medicine, and ethics. It aims to provide a forum to exchange ideas in order to protect public health, reduce health disparities, promote quality of care, and facilitate dialogue on emerging science. ASMLE publishes two journals, the *Journal* of *Law, Medicine & Ethics* and the *American Journal of Law & Medicine*, which cover all aspects of law, ethics, and medicine, including issues related to assisted suicide and euthanasia.

The Center for Bioethics & Human Dignity (CBHD)
Trinity International University, 2065 Half Day Rd.
Deerfield, IL   60015
(847) 317-8180 • fax: (847) 317-8101
e-mail: info@cbhd.org
website: www.cbhd.org

The Center for Bioethics & Human Dignity (CBHD) is a Christian bioethics research organization. It opposes abortion, assisted suicide, and euthanasia and publishes research in support of its positions. Articles and podcasts are available on the CBHD website, including the article "Euthanasia: Who Needs It?"

Compassion & Choices
PO Box 101810, Denver, CO   80250
(800) 247-7421 • fax: (866) 312-2690
website: www.compassionandchoices.org

Compassion & Choices is the largest organization in the United States advocating for patients' rights at the end of life, including the right to assisted suicide. Compassion & Choices provides clients with information, educates the public and health care professionals about end-of-life decision making, and advocates for choice at the end of life. Compassion & Choices offers many documents on end-of-life issues, including assisted suicide, at its website, including "The Aid-in-Dying Movement."

Disability Rights Education & Defense Fund (DREDF)
3075 Adeline St., Ste. 210, Berkeley, CA   94703
(510) 644-2555 • fax: (510) 841-8645
e-mail: info@dredf.org
website: www.dredf.org

Disability Rights Education & Defense Fund is a national civil rights law and policy center directed by individuals with disabilities and parents who have children with disabilities. DREDF works to advance the civil and human rights of people with disabilities through legal advocacy, training, education, and public policy and legislative development. DREDF has several publications available at its website, including *Why Assisted Suicide Must Not Be Legalized.*

Ethics and Public Policy Center (EPPC)
1730 M St. NW, Ste. 910, Washington, DC   20036
(202) 682-1200 • fax: (202) 408-0632
e-mail: ethics@eppc.org
website: www.eppc.org

The Ethics and Public Policy Center states that its purpose is to promote the application of "the Judeo-Christian moral tradition to critical issues of public policy." Through its core programs, such as Bioethics and American Democracy, EPPC and its scholars work to promote a larger role for religion in public policy. EPPC publishes *The New Atlantis,* a quarterly journal about technology with an emphasis on bioethics.

Euthanasia Research & Guidance Organization (ERGO)
24829 Norris Ln., Junction City, OR   97448-9559
(541) 998-1873
e-mail: ergo@efn.org
website: www.assistedsuicide.org

The Euthanasia Research & Guidance Organization is a nonprofit organization that believes voluntary euthanasia, physician-assisted suicide, and self-deliverance are all appropriate life endings depending on the individual medical and ethical circumstances. ERGO develops and publishes guidelines—ethical, psychological and legal—for patients and physicians to prepare them to make life-ending decisions. Available at the ERGO website are videos, books, and essays, including the essay "Liberty and Death: A Manifesto Concerning an Individual's Right to Choose to Die."

The Hastings Center

21 Malcolm Gordon Rd., Garrison, NY   10524-4125
(845) 424-4040 • fax: (845) 424-4545
e-mail: mail@thehastingscenter.org
website: www.thehastingscenter.org

The Hastings Center is a nonprofit bioethics research institute that works to address fundamental ethical issues in the areas of health, medicine, and the environment as they affect individuals, communities, and societies. The center conducts research and education and collaborates with policy makers to identify and analyze the ethical dimensions of their work. The organization publishes two periodicals: the *Hastings Center Report* and *IRB: Ethics & Human Research.*

Human Life International (HLI)

4 Family Life Ln., Front Royal, VA   22630
(800) 549-5433 • fax: (540) 622-6247
e-mail: hli@hli.org
website: www.hli.org

Human Life International is a Roman Catholic organization that describes itself as the largest international pro-life organization in the world. With affiliates and associates in over one hundred countries, HLI trains, organizes, and equips pro-life leaders around the world. HLI publishes the monthly newsletters *Mission Report* and *FrontLines*, as well as research articles, among which is "Lexicon: Euthanasia."

Patients Rights Council

PO Box 760, Steubenville, OH   43952
(800) 958-5678
website: www.patientsrightscouncil.org

The Patients Rights Council is a nonprofit educational and research organization that addresses euthanasia, assisted suicide, and end-of-life issues from a public policy perspective. The council builds and maintains strong networks with individuals and groups to influence policy and news coverage. The organization provides educational research and materials at its website, including "Euthanasia, Assisted Suicide, and Health Care Decisions: Protecting Yourself and Your Family."

Physicians for Compassionate Care Education Foundation
PO Box 1933, Yakima, WA   98907
(503) 533-8154
e-mail: physiciansforcompassionatecare@verizon.net
website: www.pccef.org

Physicians for Compassionate Care Education Foundation is an association of physicians and other health professionals who are opposed to assisted suicide. Physicians for Compassionate Care works to educate the medical profession and the public to the dangers of euthanasia and physician-assisted suicide. The group publishes videos, articles, and a quarterly newsletter, all available at its website.

Bibliography

Books

Nan Bauer-Maglin and Donna Perry
Final Acts: Death, Dying, and the Choices We Make. New Brunswick, NJ: Rutgers University Press, 2010.

Mark F. Carr, ed.
Physician Assisted Suicide: A Variety of Religious Perspectives. Tucson, AZ: Wheatmark, 2008.

Lewis M. Cohen
No Good Deed: A Story of Medicine, Murder Accusations, and the Debate over How We Die. New York: HarperCollins, 2010.

William H. Colby
Unplugged: Reclaiming Our Right to Die in America. New York: American Management Association, 2008.

Tim Falconer
That Good Night: Ethicists, Euthanasia, and the End-of-Life Care. Toronto: Penguin Canada, 2009.

Elizabeth Price Foley
The Law of Life and Death. Cambridge, MA: Harvard University Press, 2011.

Neil M. Gorsuch
The Future of Assisted Suicide and Euthanasia. Princeton, NJ: Princeton University Press, 2009.

Penney Lewis
Assisted Dying and Legal Change. New York: Oxford University Press, 2007.

Guenter Lewy   *Assisted Death in Europe and America: Four Regimes and Their Lessons.* New York: Oxford University Press, 2011.

John B. Mitchell   *Understanding Assisted Suicide: Nine Issues to Consider.* Ann Arbor: University of Michigan Press, 2007.

Craig Paterson   *Assisted Suicide and Euthanasia: A Natural Law Ethics Approach.* Burlington, VT: Ashgate, 2008.

Lila Perl   Cruzan v. Missouri: *The Right to Die?* Tarrytown, NY: Marshall Cavendish Benchmark, 2008.

Wesley J. Smith   *Forced Exit: Euthanasia, Assisted Suicide, and the New Duty to Die.* New York: Encounter Books, 2006.

Michael Stingl   *The Price of Compassion: Assisted Suicide and Euthanasia.* Buffalo, NY: Broadview Press, 2010.

Mary Warnock and Elisabeth Macdonald   *Easeful Death: Is There a Case for Assisted Dying?* New York: Oxford University Press, 2008.

Robert Young   *Medically Assisted Death.* Cambridge: Cambridge University Press, 2007.

Periodicals and Internet Sources

Jacob M. Appel   "A Suicide Right for the Mentally Ill? A Swiss Case Opens a New Debate," *Hastings Center Report*, May/June 2007.

Julian Baggini	"Suicide Can Be a Rational Choice," *Independent* (London), February 27, 2010.
Daniel Bergner	"Death in the Family," *New York Times Magazine*, December 2, 2007.
Lee Black and Robert M. Sade	"Lethal Injection and Physicians: State Law vs. Medical Ethics," *JAMA: Journal of the American Medical Association*, December 19, 2007.
Dave Bohon	"Legalized Suicide: What the Numbers Don't Tell Us," *New American*, March 15, 2011.
Thomas A. Bowden	"After Ten Years, States Still Resist Assisted Suicide," *Objective Standard*, October 30, 2007.
Daniel Callahan	"Organized Obfuscation: Advocacy for Physician-Assisted Suicide," *Hastings Center Report*, September/October 2008.
Ross Douthat	"A More Perfect Death," *New York Times*, September 7, 2009.
Marie Jeanne Ferrari	"Is There an Alternative to Euthanasia?," *Catholic Insight*, November 2008.
Ilora Finlay	"Assisted Suicide Is Fine in a Perfect World. We Don't Live (or Die) in One," *Times* (London), April 1, 2009.
Kathleen M. Foley	"Is Physician-Assisted Suicide Ever Acceptable? It's Never Acceptable," *Family Practice News*, June 1, 2007.

Atul Gawande "Letting Go: What Should Medicine Do When It Can't Save Your Life?," *New Yorker*, August 2, 2010.

Max Hastings "My 96-Year-Old Mother Wanted to End Her Life. But I Still Believe Assisted Suicide Is a Path to Barbarity," *Daily Mail* (London), February 6, 2010.

Herbert Hendin and Kathleen Foley "Physician Assisted Suicide: A Medical Perspective," *Michigan Law Review*, June 2008.

Richard Huxtable "Mercy Killings: It Is Time to Address the Legal Lottery," *Nursing Times*, February 9, 2010.

Leon R. Kass "The Right to Life and Human Dignity," *New Atlantis*, Spring 2007.

Cathleen Kaveny "'Peaceful and Private': Montana's Supreme Court Rules on Assisted Suicide," *Commonweal*, March 12, 2010.

Jean Kutner "Tending to the Dying in Hospitals," *Denver Post*, February 18, 2009.

Kathryn Jean Lopez "In Revolt Against Euthanasia," Townhall.com, September 25, 2009. http://townhall.com.

Rita L. Marker and Wesley J. Smith "When Killing Yourself Isn't Suicide," *National Review*, March 5, 2007.

Mickey Maurer   "Live Like Humans and Die Like Dogs," *Indianapolis Business Journal*, August 10, 2009.

Timothy E. Quill   "Is Physician-Assisted Suicide Ever Acceptable? It's Justified in Rare Cases," *Family Practice News*, June 1, 2007.

Isaac Sakinofsky   "Rational Suicide and the Older Adult: A Humane Experiment Gone Adrift," *CrossCurrents*, Summer 2008.

Margaret Somerville   "When Is Euthanasia Justified?," *Globe & Mail* (Toronto), March 15, 2010.

Robert Steinbrook   "Physician-Assisted Death—from Oregon to Washington State," *New England Journal of Medicine*, December 11, 2008.

Cal Thomas   "A Right to Die?," Townhall.com, August 4, 2009. http://townhall.com.

Kathryn L. Tucker   "At the Very End of Life: The Emergence of Policy Supporting Aid in Dying Among Mainstream Medical and Health Policy Associations," *Harvard Health Policy Review*, Spring 2009.

Edward Turner   "A Real Choice at the End of Life for People Who Are Desperate," *Independent on Sunday* (London), December 14, 2008.

A.N. Wilson   "I Still Wish That I Had Killed My
                   Darling Mother," *Daily Mail*
                   (London), September 24, 2009.

Index